C000082207

HALF CAB

TWILIGHT

Stewart J Brown

Capital Transport

First published 2001
ISBN 1 85414 240 2
Published by Capital Transport Publishing,
38 Long Elmes, Harrow Weald, Middlesex
Designed by Tim Demuth
Printed by CS Graphics, Singapore

Half Cab . . .

CONTENTS

Warrington was the biggest user of Foden double-deckers, although its Foden fleet only totalled 14. All postwar Fodens had concealed radiators, anticipating the trend to come in the 1950s. New in 1949, this is one of five PVD6s with East Lancs bodies delivered that year. A later East Lancs bodied Foden follows, partially obscured by a Wolseley car. Geoff Lumb

THE INITIAL idea behind this book was to chronicle the demise of the British half-cab double-decker. The last, a Leyland Titan PD3, entered service in November 1969, so there was a clearly defined end date.

The start date was more problematic. The first production Leyland Atlanteans entered service in December 1958 – and it was the Atlantean which brought about a rethink on double-deck bus design and ultimately rendered the front-engined half-cab model obsolete. Development work on what became the Atlantean started earlier in the decade, so this volume begins with an overview of the bus industry in the early part of the 1950s before looking in greater detail at the changes which

took place in bus design and in operators' purchases of urban buses in the period between 1958 and 1969.

No account of the demise of the half-cab would be complete if it didn't examine the reasons for this, and looked at the models which were ousting familiar front-engined chassis from operators' orders.

Initially these were rear-engined double-deckers – the Atlantean and the Fleetline – but the 1960s saw an upsurge of interest in one-man-operation (this was a time when women bus drivers were rare indeed) and with it a switch towards rear-engined single-deckers. This was prompted by two major challenges facing operators. Firstly, passenger numbers were falling and fares increases only accelerated the move away from public transport to private cars. Therefore costs had to be cut. And secondly, in many parts of the country the recruitment of drivers and conductors was difficult. The combination of shift working and relatively low basic wage rates saw many big urban operators recruiting staff who were ill-suited for the job, with consequent high turnover of drivers and conductors.

One-man-operation promised higher wages for those drivers working such schedules, a lower wage bill in total for the operator, and a

Left **One of the classic half-cab designs of the postwar era was the combination of Leyland's Titan PD2 chassis with Leyland's own bodywork. Ribble was a major customer, taking 225 between 1948 and 1952. Most had lowbridge bodies, but 40 delivered in 1948–49 were of highbridge layout, as seen here in Fleetwood. It is a testament to Leyland's durability and Ribble's maintenance than when these buses were sold in the early 1960s all but a few saw further service with independents.** Paul Caudell

Lowheight contrast. The most-successful of lowheight bus designs, the Bristol Lodekka (right) is seen in Glasgow alongside one of the least successful, the Albion Lowlander. The Lowlander had a Northern Counties body which helped disguise the model's high-driving position and was operated by Western SMT, the biggest user of the Lowlander. The FLF Lodekka was in the Central SMT fleet. Stewart J Brown

reduction in the number of people employed in an industry which was permanently short of staff anyway. Until 1966 only single-deck buses could be operated by one person. There was trade union resistance to one-man-operation in many places, as there was to the introduction of bigger buses. But change was coming, and with it came the end of the half-cab double-decker.

That it took over ten years for the half-cab to disappear from operators' orders (compare that with the speedy adoption of low-floor buses in the second half of the 1990s) reflects a number of conflicting factors. There was the issue of cost. Rear-engined buses were more expensive to buy – and it quickly became clear they were more expensive to operate as well,

ABERDEEN CORPORATION
TRANSPORT DEPARTMENT

TIME TABLE
FARE TABLE
STREET DIRECTORY
ROUTE MAP

with higher fuel and maintenance bills. They were less reliable too.

Front-engined buses were proven, easy to maintain and reliable in service (with just a few exceptions). With a forward-entrance body on a 30ft-long chassis they carried only six fewer passengers than a rear-engined model and offered passengers a similar standard of travelling environment – that is to say an enclosed saloon with some warmth, rather than an open rear platform with its draughts. Incidentally, throughout this book in describing entrance layouts I have used the generally accepted distinction forward and front to differentiate between an entrance behind the front axle (forward entrance) as on Leyland Titans or AEC Regents, or ahead of it (front entrance) as on Atlanteans and Fleetlines.

Many operators of front-engined buses specified a manual transmission. That might mean frequent clutch replacement in an urban fleet, but the gearbox was generally unbreakable. Doubts existed in some quarters about the durability and repairability of fluid transmissions which were standard on the Atlantean and Fleetline.

And even within operators there could be conflicting views. The traffic department might be keen to run modern high-capacity rear-engined buses on busy routes, while the chief engineer would be arguing that to maintain a high level of vehicle availability and to keep maintenance costs down, front-engined buses were the only choice.

These were interesting times, when municipal managers could still get bespoke bodies from builders such as East Lancs and Roe, or when the mighty Leyland Motors would develop models to meet the needs of major customers, such as the Panther Cub for Manchester and the Lowlander for the Scottish Bus Group – neither of which was a great success, it has to be said.

Two approaches to the low bridge problem, seen in Edinburgh in 1963. Nearest the camera is a 1951 AEC Regent III, which has a side-gangway lowbridge body by Burlingham of a design clearly related to Ribble's White Lady coaches of the same period. Behind it a 1961 Bristol Lodekka approaches, its low-frame chassis allowing the use of a centre gangway in both decks. The Lodekka is an LD6G and has Cave-Browne-Cave heating with its distinctive radiators on either side of the destination display. Both buses belong to Scottish Omnibuses and are seen in Edinburgh's St Andrew Square bus station in 1963. *Geoff Lumb*

I've tried to illustrate a broad cross-section of the vehicles in operation when the first Atlanteans took to Britain's streets, and of the new buses delivered in the period when the archetypally British half-cab double-decker was slowly disappearing from the production lines at Southall, Leyland, Wolverhampton, Guildford and Coventry. Very few of the photographs have been published before.

In writing a story such as this one is indebted to those who have explored specific areas of possible interest and reported on them in magazines such as *Bus & Coach* and *Buses Illustrated,* as well as to the active volunteers in the PSV Circle whose records provide any transport author with a wealth of data.

My thanks also go to those photographers who have so willingly provided valuable original colour transparencies and whose work is credited individually throughout the book. Those credited to Chris Aston and Martin Llewellyn were supplied by Omnicolour. Thanks, too, to my old friends John Aldridge and Alan Townsin, who kindly commented on drafts of the text, and to David Berry, Alan Gurley, Brian Hirst, Peter Iddon, Roy Marshall and Alan Martin who in conversation have provided additional items of information which have enhanced the story.

Much of this story is set in the 1960s – the Swinging Sixties. And what made the '60s swing was pop music. The chapter

titles all come from number one hits of the period, some of which show a real sympathy among pop musicians with the problems facing operators struggling to cope with the new generation of rear-engined buses which were slowly ousting the trusty half-cabs.

Stewart J Brown
Reedley Hallows, 2001

Top **There was a period in the 1960s when sales of low-frame single-deckers, such as this Leyland Panther operated by Hull Corporation, seriously depressed demand for new double-deckers. Standee single-deckers generally carried more people than the 15-year-old half cab double-deckers they were replacing. Roe built the body to a design similar to that used by Park Royal on single-deckers for Manchester.** Chris Aston

Above **Relatively small numbers of new double-deck chassis in the late 1940s and early 1950s were fitted with older bodies transferred from prewar buses. Among the most unusual were two Bristol K6G chassis which entered service with Silcox of Pembroke Dock in 1952 which had 1940 Metro-Cammell bodies. These had originally been fitted to Leyland trolleybuses operated by Birmingham City Transport.** Maurice Bateman

The early 1950s

SETTING THE SCENE

WHEN Leyland launched its Titan TD1 in 1927, it set the shape for double-deck buses for the following 30 years.

The TD-series Titans set new standards for double-deck bus design by combining a relatively low frame with a driving position alongside the engine. Some of the Titan's features had been seen before, but Leyland packaged them in a way which marked a significant advance on previous designs.

The driver generally sat in a half-width cab, although from the mid-1930s in a few fleets such as Blackpool, Bournemouth and Lytham St Annes, a full-width cab was fitted to add symmetry (and, it might be argued, modernity) to the appearance of what was in truth a rather odd-looking vehicle.

By the 1950s TD1 Titans were few and far between (except perhaps on Jersey), but a goodly number of later prewar buses were still in regular service. The Second World War had prolonged their lives, and Titans from the mid-1930s could still be found in most parts of the country, along with contemporary AEC Regents, Bristols and Daimlers. There were also smaller numbers of prewar Crossleys (most notably in the Manchester Corporation fleet until 1957) and Albions (with Glasgow Corporation until 1956).

Some smaller fleets managed to replace prewar models quite quickly – all had gone in Barrow by 1951 and in Wallasey by 1952, for example. But in other places they lingered on,

not only into the late 1950s, but on in to the 1960s too. The last prewar buses came out of service in Birmingham in 1957; in Manchester in 1962 and with Alexander (Midland) in 1964.

Wartime models had varied lives, largely because of the poor quality of the timber used in the construction of their bodywork. Some were sold soon after peace was declared. Blackburn Corporation, for example, sold two Guy Arabs in 1947 when they were just four years old. That they saw no further service as PSVs is a strong indictment of their Pickering bodies.

Some municipal fleets went in for rebodying of wartime or late prewar buses – Belfast and Glasgow corporations are prime examples – and these generally lasted into the 1960s. A number of BET fleets also chose to rebody prewar buses in the late 1940s – most notably Ribble and Southdown. The latter had significant numbers of mid- and late-1930s Titans so treated, while Ribble had over 130 TD-series Titans rebodied by Alexander,

Facing page **Leyland's original TD1 Titan revolutionised double-deck bus design. The concept survived for almost 50 years with refinements as time passed by. The postwar PD2 was the most successful model to carry the Titan name. This is a 1957 example operated by Edinburgh Corporation. It has Metro-Cammell Orion bodywork.** Harry Hay

Top right **From 1936 to 1965 all new buses for Blackpool Corporation had fully-fronted bodywork. Its first postwar purchases were two batches of Leyland Titan PD2/5s with exuberant Burlingham bodies which seated 52 passengers and had centre entrances. These unusual buses were withdrawn in the second half of the 1960s, their replacements being rather more prosaic rear-entrance PD3s.** Geoff Lumb

Centre right **Prewar buses were still around in large numbers in the mid-1950s and examples which were well looked after by their original owners found ready buyers among small independents. New to Ribble in 1937, this Titan TD4 had a 1947 Burlingham body and was sold in 1957 to Simonds of Botesdale who ran it until 1963.** Frank Mussett

Bottom right **There were really only two major variations in wartime double-deck bodywork – highbridge or lowbridge. This is a Duple lowbridge body on a Daimler CWA6 in the Widnes Corporation fleet. Widnes received six Daimlers in 1945. Four were withdrawn in 1963-64 while the other two which had been fitted with new East Lancs bodies in 1954 lasted until 1967–68.** Geoff Lumb

Facing page top **Wartime buses – this is a 1945 West Bridgford Daimler CWA6 with Brush body – were often short-lived because of bodywork problems. However some ran right through the 1950s and a few, generally after substantial rebuilding, survived into the mid-1960s. This bus was a late survivor and was one of the last CWA6s in service when it was withdrawn in 1967. It is seen in Nottingham; Nottingham City Transport took over the operation of West Bridgford's 28-strong bus fleet in 1968.** Chris Aston

Facing page bottom **In the late 1940s and early 1950s a number of major fleets extended the lives of prewar buses by having them rebodied. Among BET companies, Ribble, Southdown and East Kent carried out extensive rebodying programmes on prewar Titans. This is an East Kent TD4, with a new lowbridge ECW body.** Frank Mussett

Right **Belfast Corporation undertook a major rebodying programme in the mid-1950s. It bought 100 Daimler CWA6s from London Transport in 1953–54, all of which were fitted with new bodies by local coachbuilder Harkness in 1955–56. This followed the similar rebodying of 42 of Belfast's own CWA6s earlier in the decade. Belfast got its money's worth out of the London Daimlers – all 100 were still on the road when this one was photographed in 1969, its chassis then 23 years old.** Alan Mortimer

Bottom right **Some rebuilds were more convincing than others. At first glance this Guy could pass for an Arab IV. But it is in fact an ex-London Transport Arab II, its 1945 origins effectively disguised by the new registration and a 1954 Northern Counties body. The high driving position gives the game away to those who know. It was one of 10 operated by Western SMT, and is seen on the Isle of Bute.** Harry Hay

Burlingham and ECW in the period 1947–50. And many fleets simply went in for major rebuilds which generally guaranteed a life approaching the postwar industry standard of 15 years or thereabouts. The Tilling group undertook major rebuilds of both bodies and chassis on prewar buses.

There was a postwar boom in new bus buying. This was in part because of a rapid increase in passenger numbers, but was mainly the result of a slow-down in deliveries during the war and the fact that many time-expired prewar buses were still in daily service.

Leyland and AEC re-emerged as the key players in the first ten years after the war, with the Titan PD1 and PD2 and the Regent

II and III respectively. By the end of 1955 AEC had delivered 8,500 Regents to UK fleets, over half of which went to London Transport. Other big Regent buyers in this period included some of the larger municipals such as Glasgow, Leeds, Liverpool and Newcastle, as well as a number of BET and Scottish Omnibuses group subsidiaries.

Leyland supplied some 8,700 Titans in the same period of which almost 2,200 were for LT. The Titan was a popular choice with fleets large and small, from Inverness to the Isle of Wight. A large number of operators built up big fleets of the original postwar PD1 model. Manchester Corporation was the biggest user with 200, while Central SMT had well over 100. Tilling group companies took the best part of 200 in 1947–48, and even London Transport had 65. The PD2 which succeeded it didn't sell to Tilling companies but was bought by a very large number of other fleets. In 1950, for example, over 60 different companies took delivery of PD2 Titans ranging from ones and twos for small operators such as King Alfred in Winchester and AA in Ayr, through to 50 or more for Birmingham City Transport, Leicester Corporation and Ribble. Many Titans of this period had Leyland's own bodywork.

Bristol was supplying its traditional Tilling group customers, but between 1946 and 1948

Top left **UK deliveries of Leyland's Titan averaged around 1,150 a year in the period up to 1950 and peaked at almost 1,700 in 1949 and 1950. Many Titans had Leyland's own bodywork, as fitted to this 1950 PD2 operated by Seaview Services on the Isle of Wight. The Southern Vectis Bristol Lodekka in the background shows an early style of grille with the mouldings carried down to enclose the number plate.** David Brown

Centre left **London Transport's RT-class Regents had long lives. Many were sold prematurely in the late 1950s, being snapped up quickly by independents, while others lasted in LT service until the end of the 1970s. This is a newly-overhauled bus in 1967, photographed at a time when most operators of Regent IIIs were selling them for scrap rather than overhauling them for continued service.** Geoff Rixon

Left **New bus deliveries hit a peak in 1950 and Yorkshire Traction in that year added 35 Leyland Titan PD2/3s to its fleet. These had 56-seat Roe bodies and they replaced prewar Titans. Withdrawal of the 1950 Titans started in 1962 and was completed in 1964 – yet half-a-dozen PS2 Tigers which had been delivered at the same time as the Titans, but had presumably been less hard-worked, had their lives extended in 1963 by being rebodied as double-deckers.** Geoff Lumb

Right **The classic combination of Bristol K-series chassis and ECW lowbridge bodywork could be seen throughout England and Wales. This is a 1953 KSW6B operated by Thames Valley which was the last Tilling group company to buy lowbridge K-series, staying with the type until 1955.**
Gerald Mead

Below **Prior to the nationalisation of Bristol, the K was chosen by a few municipal fleets. These included Pontypridd, an operation not that far from the Bristol factory, which took 10. Six-bay bodywork was rare after World War 2, but that was the layout adopted by Beadle for the Pontypridd Bristols. This is a K6G delivered in 1950, the last year in which Pontypridd took Bristols – its next new buses, in 1956, were Guys.** Martin Llewellyn

200 new K-types – just over 20 per cent of Bristol's output of double-deckers – went to fleets outside the Tilling group. The biggest user, taking 100 over that three year period (and 143 in total by 1950) was BET subsidiary Maidstone & District. Small numbers were supplied to London Transport in 1946 (the residue of a wartime allocation) and a few were bought by municipalities: Aberdare, Cardiff, Doncaster, Luton, Merthyr Tydfil,

Pontypridd, Rotherham, St Helens and Stockton. There were four engine options. The first postwar model was the K6A with an AEC 7.7-litre engine, but from 1946 Bristol's own new AVW engine was offered in the K6B, along with the Gardner 5LW (K5G) and Gardner 6LW (K6G). As these models came on stream in increasing numbers K6A production ceased. The last entered service with Maidstone & District in 1950, which had been one of the biggest users of the type.

The nationalisation of the Tilling group's bus interests in 1948 included Bristol (and the ECW bodybuilding business) and the last few non-Tilling Bristols entered service in 1950, apart from two K6G models which were not put into operation until 1952 by Silcox of Pembroke Dock.

Bristol remained a major force in the supply of double-deckers but, under the terms of the 1947 Transport Act, only to operators which were part of the new British Transport Commission, set up in 1948 by the Labour Government: in effect London Transport, and the Tilling and Scottish Omnibuses groups.

Daimler maintained a strong presence in municipal fleets. Birmingham was easily the biggest user, putting over 450 Daimlers into service between 1947 and 1950. Other important Daimler users were Coventry, Liverpool, Manchester and Salford. However Daimler double-deck sales outside the municipal sector were relatively low at around two dozen a year in the late 1940s. Daimler's

Above **Around 20 per cent of postwar Bristol K production went to operators outside the Tilling group. Rotherham Corporation, which built up a fleet of 28 postwar Ks, was the last major non-Tilling operator to put the type into service, in 1950. It also bought the single-deck L-series, and this bus is in fact one of eight 1949-50 L6Bs which were rebodied as double-deckers by East Lancs after just two years in service.** Martin Llewellyn

Below **Most of Derby Corporation's postwar buses came from Daimler. The body on its 1950 intake – 15 CVD6s – came from local manufacturer Brush, based in Loughborough.** Martin Llewellyn

postwar CV-series models were available with four engines. These were the Gardner 5LW and 6LW, AEC 7.7 or the Daimler CD6, and these were identified by chassis type codes CVG5, CVG6, CVA6 and CVD6 respectively. The CVA6 was short-lived; the last batch entered service in 1950 with Liverpool Corporation.

Daimler had also tried offering a more powerful model, the 150bhp CD650, which not only offered a preselector gearbox, then the Daimler standard, but had power-hydraulic brakes and power-assisted steering Only 14 entered service with British operators. The CD650 designation came from the imperial dimensions – 650 cu in – of the 10.6-litre Daimler engine.

Guy in the early postwar years won some business from operators who had clearly been impressed by its wartime Arabs. Offered with either five- or six-cylinder Gardner engines, the Arab III, introduced in 1946, had a low radiator and bonnet which might have looked more modern had it not been flanked by wings with an unusual reverse curve. Arab buyers were a mixture of municipal and company operators but the only really big users were Birmingham and Southampton corporations. Guy was in the second division alongside Dennis, while some of the other players in the double-deck market were soon to be out of the game altogether.

Crossley's main double-deck customer before the war was Manchester Corporation.

Above **The Daimler CD650 was a rare vehicle indeed, with just 14 being delivered to British operators. It had a 10.6-litre Daimler engine and was easily identifiable by its large radiator. Blue Bus of Willington ran four with lowbridge Willowbrook bodies which were fitted with platform doors.** Geoff Lumb

Below **The Guy Arab III had a low-set radiator and distinctive wings with a reverse curve on the** leading edge. Home market deliveries of double-deck Arabs were averaging around 200 a year between 1946 and 1950, with buyers including Chesterfield Corporation which in 1950 took 20 with Gardner 6LW engines and lowbridge Weymann bodies. 1950 was in fact Guy's best postwar year for double-deck deliveries, when 350 entered service – from there it was all downhill. A Chesterfield Crossley can be seen in the background. Martin Llewellyn

bodywork until 1958. Its last major contract comprised 90 bodies for Glasgow Corporation on BUT trolleybus chassis.

Dennis was building Lances in small numbers – precisely 100 between 1947 and 1954. The main buyers were Aldershot & District with 72 and Lancashire United with 19. Albion's Venturer was bought by Glasgow Corporation and by a few fleets in South Wales. Albion built only 220 Venturers for home-market customers after the war – 138 of these were for Glasgow and 50 for companies in the Red & White group. The last Venturers entered service in Glasgow in 1953.

Foden – which had built one double-deck prototype in 1934 – entered the fray with its PVD6 model in 1945. Two municipal fleets close to Foden's Cheshire factory bought the company's double-deckers – Chester (with 10) and Warrington (15) – and a few found their way to Scottish independents. But only 57 PVD6s were built for UK operation. It was, incidentally, the first double-deck chassis with a new-look front. Indeed Foden didn't offer any postwar bus or coach chassis with exposed radiators. The last PVD6 entered service with Warrington in 1956.

And mention has to be made of Atkinson which sold one double-decker to the Stalybridge, Hyde, Mossley and Dukinfield joint board in 1955. It had a Gardner 6LW engine and a centre-entrance body by Northern Counties. This body layout was favoured by just four operators in the early postwar years: the other three were Blackpool and West Hartlepool corporations and the West Riding Automobile Co. Britain's last new centre-entrance double-deckers were six Daimler CVG6s delivered to SHMD in 1956.

At this time there were still trolleybuses

Above **Manchester Corporation was the biggest buyer of Crossley's postwar DD42 double-decker, taking 291 between 1946 and 1949, which represented a quarter of Crossley's output of DD42s. All the Manchester vehicles had Crossley bodywork. This 1946 example was withdrawn in 1962; the last Manchester Crossley came out of service in 1968.** Geoff Lumb

Below **Dennis Lance production totalled just 100 postwar units when it came to an end in 1954. Aldershot & District was the biggest user with 72, and its last 32 delivered in 1954 had Gardner 5LW engines and Birmingham-style bonnets. These were the only Lances with new-look fronts. Lowbridge East Lancs bodywork was fitted to 20 of them.** Photobus

In the late 1940s and early 1950s Crossley sold just over 1,100 DD42 double-deckers to a few municipals and independents. This was a respectable figure by any standard. Manchester was once again the biggest buyer taking 291. Other fleet operators included Birmingham (260), Bolton (75), Stockport (65), Liverpool (50), and with smaller numbers Leeds, Sheffield and Portsmouth. The last DD42s entered service in 1952 with Rotherham Corporation. Crossley's engine proved disappointing, which no doubt played a major part in the absence of repeat orders from most customers. And that effectively ended Crossley as a builder of double-deck chassis, although it was later involved in the development of the AEC Bridgemaster, and would continue building double-deck

Right **The last Albion Venturers to enter service in England did so in 1950 and included three with lowbridge Strachans bodywork for South Yorkshire of Pontefract. These were CX37 models with 120bhp 9.9-litre Albion engines and Albion constant-mesh gearboxes.** Geoff Lumb

Centre right **Unique is an over-worked word, but certainly applies to this bus in the SHMD fleet. It was the only Atkinson double-decker built. The body was by Northern Counties. SHMD was the last operator to specify centre entrances on double-deckers.** Geoff Lumb

Below right **Chester Corporation briefly standardised on Foden PVD6s with Gardner 6LW engines and 56-seat Massey bodies – a true north-west of England product with the chassis produced in Sandbach, the engine in Patricroft and the body in Wigan. The last of Chester's Fodens was withdrawn in 1970.** Alan Mortimer

running for 25 municipalities and in seven of these – Bournemouth, Brighton, Huddersfield, Ipswich, Reading, South Shields and Wolverhampton – they made up over 50 per cent of the fleet.

So a vast range of pre- and postwar chassis types could be seen in the mid-1950s, along with an even wider range of bodywork – much of it from small-scale builders who disappeared when the boom turned to bust at the start of the decade. Many were primarily serving local customers. For example Welsh Metal Industries produced unimaginably austere-looking bodies for a few operators in South Wales (although a couple were exported to Scotland), while Scottish Aviation, a pioneer in the use of aluminium construction, built quite respectable looking four-bay double-deck bodies with Glasgow Corporation its only customer – taking 20 out of a total production of 21. (The 21st was a demonstration body on a Foden PVD6 which spent most of its life with Garelochhead Coach Services.)

Other relatively low-volume builders of double-deck bodies which had ceased production by the middle of the decade included companies such as Brockhouse of Clydebank selling 40 bodies to Aberdeen, Edinburgh and Glasgow corporations in 1950–51; Croft of Glasgow, with bodies for Dundee and Glasgow and the Caledonian Omnibus Co; Roberts of Wakefield, which managed a more respectable spread of orders, mainly from municipal fleets including Colchester, Glasgow and Nottingham; Brush of Loughborough and Barnard of Norwich.

Of what might be termed the mainstream double-deck bodybuilders, Massey was the smallest – with output averaging about one bus a week. East Lancs, Northern Counties and Roe were in the middle range, while Alexander, ECW, Park Royal and Metro-Cammell-Weymann were building the highest

volumes. In the late 1950s Roe's double-deck output was averaging around 190 bodies a year while Park Royal was building an average of 275 single- and double-deck bodies excluding Routemasters. Park Royal's double-deck exports (mainly on AEC Regent Vs to Teheran and Baghdad) at times outnumbered its home market sales.

MCW was best known for its ubiquitous lightweight Orion body, a popular choice with municipal fleets from Aberdeen in the north to Plymouth in the south. Opinions varied on its appearance, with some observers criticising the use of shallow windows for the upper deck and deep windows on the lower deck. And in pursuit of low weight the basic Orion could be very basic indeed. MCW's claim that "its light weight has been achieved without sacrifice of passenger comfort or skimping of the specification in any way" is one that was open to argument.

The highly-standardised Orion would enjoy a long production run from 1954 to 1968 and was fitted to all conventional double-deck chassis of the period – AEC Regent, Daimler CV-series, Guy Arab and Leyland Titan.

Such was the scene when Leyland's Lowloader prototype first took to the streets in 1954 and it's difficult to imagine the effect it must have had. It appeared in a Britain where every double-decker built over the previous 25 years – apart from the side-engined AEC Q – owed something to Leyland's revolutionary Titan of 1927.

Above **Massey was the smallest builder of double-deck bus bodies in the late 1950s and early 1960s, with output averaging around one bus a week. Birkenhead Corporation standardised on the combination of Massey body on exposed-radiator PD2 chassis, buying little else between 1957 and 1967. This bus may have looked old-fashioned when compared with the Atlanteans entering service on the other side of the Mersey with Liverpool Corporation, but it did capture something of the spirit of a well-run municipal transport department with its distinctive livery, smart appearance and generous destination displays.** A Moyes

Facing page above **Daimler was a popular municipal choice. This is a 1954 Halifax CVG6 which illustrates that Metro-Cammell's oft-criticised Orion body could look attractive in the right livery. The Halifax colour scheme was inspired by a Glasgow-liveried AEC demonstrator in 1929.** Chris Aston

Facing page below **The unique combination of the MCW group's Orion body and Bristol K chassis could be found in operation with Maidstone & District. This 1945 K6A originally had the high-mounted radiator which was a characteristic feature of the wartime K-series. M&D had 25 chassis modified with the postwar style of low-mounted radiator and fitted with new Weymann bodywork in 1954.** Harry Hay

The Atlantean era

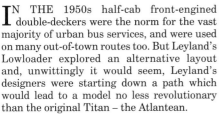

STRANGER IN PARADISE

IN THE 1950s half-cab front-engined double-deckers were the norm for the vast majority of urban bus services, and were used on many out-of-town routes too. But Leyland's Lowloader explored an alternative layout and, unwittingly it would seem, Leyland's designers were starting down a path which would lead to a model no less revolutionary than the original Titan – the Atlantean.

The rationale behind the Lowloader was, as its name implied, height reduction. The lowest easily achievable height for a double-deck bus was 13ft 6in, made possible by having a sunken upper deck gangway located on the offside of the saloon. It was an inconvenient arrangement on two counts.

For travellers on the top deck (where, incidentally, smoking was still permitted in the 1950s) there were rows of four-passenger bench seats which were awkward to get in and out of when the bus was full. And for those lower-deck travellers sitting on the offside of the bus there was the ever-present danger of bumping their heads on the sunken gangway – which intruded into the lower saloon – as they

rose out of their seats to get off the bus. Most operators fitted warning notices – classically with the wording "Mind your head" – on the backs of the offside lower-deck seats.

Bristol had addressed this problem as early as 1949 with its prototype Lodekka, which used a complex transmission with the drive ultimately taken by separate propeller shafts to each rear wheel. A lowered chassis frame allowed the gangway in the centre of the lower deck to be dropped a few inches. This, and the use of minimum headroom in both decks, produced what became known generally as the lowheight double-decker, as against the side-gangway lowbridge type.

Prototype Lodekka LDX001 entered service with Bristol Tramways and was followed in 1950 by LDX002 for the West Yorkshire Road Car Co. This bus had a single propeller shaft driving an offset differential on a rear axle with a sunken centre section, and it set the standard for the production models which would follow. Both buses had Bristol AVW engines and 58-seat bodies by Eastern Coach Works. They also had huge radiators

which gave them an ungainly appearance, in stark contrast to the neat K-series double-decker which was Bristol's standard model at the time.

The Lowloader or PDR1 was Leyland's approach to a lowheight bus. It had the engine located transversely at the rear and driving a drop-centre rear axle. This eliminated the need for a propeller shaft running from the front of the bus, which was one of the main obstacles to lowering the floor level on a double-decker with a front-mounted engine and rear-wheel drive. Instead of using the O.600 unit which powered its established Titan PD2, Leyland chose the O.350 which was smaller (and lighter) and which therefore took up less space on the platform. It was located in the offside corner so that it was partly under the staircase. This was rearward-ascending, which was something of a novelty on a rear-entrance bus.

The Lowloader had independent front suspension and a platform-type chassis in place of the conventional ladder frame. A Wilson pre-selector gearbox was fitted. The O.350 engine was turbocharged, which upped its power output from 90 to 115bhp. The concept of using a small turbocharged engine to power a double-deck bus had been tested by Leyland using a 1939 TD6 purchased from Birmingham City Transport and which spent some 12 months in 1953–54 running for Edinburgh Corporation.

The first Lowloader was bodied by Saunders-Roe and registered STF90. The 61-seat (37 up, 24 down) body was of full-front design, making Leyland's new prototype look

Left **The bus that set a design revolution in train: the first of Leyland's Lowloader prototypes, STF90 with Saunders-Roe bodywork. After a period as a demonstrator it was sold to Lowland Motorways of Glasgow in 1957, along with the second prototype, XTC684. Both ran for the company for a little over six months before being sold, and only this vehicle received Lowland livery.** Geoff Morant

Facing page **The second of Leyland's Lowloader prototypes appeared in 1954 and was also operated by Lowland Motorways in 1957. It is seen in 1966 in the ownership of Buckmaster of Leighton Buzzard. Entry to the cab was by a sliding door in the front bulkhead. Metro-Cammell built the body.** Maurice Bateman

Right At the start of the 1950s all Titans had exposed radiators, and this remained an option until production ceased in 1969. This is a 1951 PD2/12 with 58-seat Leyland Farington bodywork in operation with Maidstone & District. It was one of 53 PD2s delivered to the company in that year, the last of which were withdrawn in 1970. Leyland ceased body manufacture in 1954. David Brown

The second of Leyland's Lowloader prototypes appeared in 1954 and was also operated by Lowland Motorways in 1957. It is seen in 1966 in the ownership of Buckmaster of Leighton Buzzard. Entry to the cab was by a sliding door in the front bulkhead. Metro-Cammell built the body. Maurice Bateman

like a trolleybus without booms. Saunders-Roe was in some ways an odd choice of builder whose main experience of building double-deckers was the supply of 300 bodies on RT chassis to London Transport. However Leyland may have been attracted by its pioneering work in the use of lightweight aluminium alloy construction. The first Lowloader weighed just 6 tons 11 cwt unladen which was more than a ton lighter than a Titan PD2 with Leyland bodywork.

STF90 had the last double-deck body to be built by Saunders-Roe, and it had styling features which echoed the company's contemporary single-deck body, most commonly associated with Leyland's Tiger Cub. It was completed in 1953 and entered service in the summer of 1954, demonstrating to a number of BET fleets including Aldershot & District, City of Oxford, Devon General, East Kent, Maidstone & District, PMT, Ribble, South Wales Transport and Southdown, and also to the Ulster Transport Authority and Newcastle, Reading and Walsall corporations. It spent 18 months with Walsall in 1955–56, for which it was repainted in the corporation's blue livery.

It was followed in 1954 by a second prototype, which was bodied by MCW and registered XTC684. This body, also a rear-entrance 61-seater, was of half-cab design and was in some ways more strikingly different than STF90. Until this time any half-cab bus had incorporated some form of radiator at the front; XTC684 did not, which made it particularly distinctive. Entry to the driver's cab was by way of a sliding door in the front bulkhead – there was no external access to the cab on either of the Lowloaders. This prototype was used as a test-bed by Leyland.

Both Lowloader prototypes were sold in the spring of 1957 to Lowland Motorways of Glasgow, giving that small operator the unlikely distinction of being the first in Britain to own rear-engined double-deck buses. They only operated with Lowland until the end of that year, when both were sold to Glasgow dealer Millburn Motors – just weeks before Lowland was taken over by Scottish Omnibuses in January 1958. Both found buyers in England, and STF90 survived in service till 1963, while XTC684 lasted until 1969. STF90 was scrapped; XTC684 is awaiting restoration in the collection of the British Commercial Vehicle Museum.

When the Lowloaders were being developed, the maximum permitted length of a two-axle double-decker was 27ft. That changed in July 1956, with a new maximum of 30ft being allowed, accompanied by an increase in permitted gross vehicle weight from 12 to 14 tons. Leyland's engineers, in conjunction with those from MCW, took advantage of this to produce a 30ft-long rear-engined model which appeared in prototype form at that year's Earls Court Commercial Motor Show It had an MCW body which was integrated with the platform-type chassis.

Thus was born the Atlantean.

This semi-integral prototype had many of the features which would soon be recognised throughout the industry. Gone was the O.350 engine. In its place Leyland used the O.600 which powered its Titan. Gone, too, was the idea of retaining a rear entrance. The Atlantean had a front overhang which was long enough to allow an entrance opposite the driver. However it retained the drop-centre rear axle and independent front suspension of the original Lowloader prototypes. Overall height was just 13ft 3in and unladen weight 7 tons 16cwt 1qr – more than a ton heavier than the shorter Lowloaders but still broadly comparable with conventional double-deckers of the day.

Other noteworthy features were the "anti-pollution roof height exhaust" to use Leyland's own description of the exhaust pipe which was routed internally up the rear of the body, and the use of the engine fan to provide heating and ventilation, which meant that no

opening windows were needed on the body. Heaters were still an option on buses at this time, as they were on many cars.

The move to a front entrance was prompted in part by considerations of passenger safety. On a typical 56-seat open-platform double-decker it was accepted that the conductor could both collect fares and keep an eye on passengers boarding and alighting. But a 30ft-long 'decker could seat in excess of 70 passengers, and operators were concerned that this was placing too great a burden on the conductor. The Atlantean layout not only overcame the potential risk of platform accidents, but it provided space for even more seats – up to 78.

The first Atlantean prototype was registered 281ATC and entered demonstration service in 1956. It ran for a number of operators including PMT and Ribble, and was inspected by Glasgow Corporation in 1958. It finally returned to Leyland where it was broken up in 1965. A second similar vehicle was used as a test-bed by Leyland, but the body was not fully trimmed and it never entered operational service. It was scrapped in 1964.

The excitement generated by the Atlantean should not be allowed to obscure Leyland's considerable success with conven-

The Metro-Cammell body on this fine Wallasey Corporation PD1 looks more like a product of the 1930s than the 1940s, an impression heightened by the ornate fleet name and generous destination display. There were 48 of these PD1s, and the last Wallasey buses of this general style were 24 PD2s delivered in 1951. Frank Mussett

tional double-deckers at this time. Its standard model from the late 1940s was the PD2 which, as mentioned earlier, used Leyland's 9.8-litre O.600 engine. Early PD2s had a four-speed synchromesh gearbox, but from 1954 Leyland's semi-automatic Pneumocyclic was available as an option and quickly became popular with the bigger urban operators, such as Glasgow Corporation. The ease of driving a bus with just two pedals made it attractive to operators replacing trams or trolleybuses and who wanted to re-train the drivers of these electrically-driven vehicles to handle motorbuses. This was a feature recog-

nised by both AEC and Daimler with their pre-selector gearboxes, where a selector pedal took the place of the normal clutch pedal. In 1956 almost 600 PD2s entered service with British operators – accounting for just over a quarter of double-deck deliveries in that year.

Leyland offered Titan buyers a choice of radiators – the traditional exposed style, or what was described as the "new-look" front (or less politely as the "tin front"). The latter had first been used in 1952 for a batch of 100 chassis being delivered to Midland Red and the layout of the vertical slats in the grille was designed to incorporate that operator's BMMO badge – the Birmingham & Midland Motor Omnibus Company being the company's full title. BMMO had pioneered the concept of having a concealed radiator on a double-deck bus as early as 1942 when it had rebuilt a prewar FEDD with a new-look front which served as a prototype for the style adopted for postwar double-deck deliveries.

Operators were divided between tradition and modernity. The new-look front certainly looked more modern, and was in line with contemporary car practice. But the built-up

bonnet assembly hindered engine access and it also impeded the driver's vision to the nearside. In some operations, problems with front brake cooling became evident on Titans with the new-look front, and the design was modified in 1956 to include additional mesh grilles below the headlamps which improved the airflow to the front hubs.

The new 30ft length limit saw Leyland stretch the Titan, increasing the wheelbase from 16ft 5in to 18ft 6in. The mechanical spec-ification was little altered – primarily borrowing from the export-series OPD2 Titan a slightly deeper and thicker chassis frame and a heavier duty rear axle – and in this form the long-wheelbase Titan was known as the PD3. It was, incidentally, only available for 8ft wide bodywork (which had been authorised in 1946), unlike the shorter PD2 which could be 7ft 6in wide.

The Titan was Britain's top-selling double-decker in the late 1950s, with annual deliveries averaging around 650, compared with under 300 for AEC's rival, the Regent. In fairness to AEC, to Regent sales have to be added the small numbers of Bridgemasters

Left **The BET Group was quick to adopt high-capacity buses. BET's Northern General group of companies started taking delivery of 30ft-long PD3 Titans in 1958. These included three with 73-seat Metro-Cammell Orion bodies for Tyneside. All of the Titans bought by Northern General and its associated companies had exposed radiators. This particular bus would form the basis of the company's Tynesider semi-normal-control rebuild in 1972, illustrated on page 108.** Gerald Mead

Below **The Bridgemaster was an integral featuring AEC running units and a steel-framed Park Royal body of rather austere appearance. Most were 30ft long. Lincoln Corporation bought four – the only AECs it ever owned – in 1962. They were 76-seaters, an unusually high capacity for a rear-entrance bus.** John Jones

The AEC Regent V was Devon General's standard double-decker, and this example in Exeter bus station has Metro-Cammell Orion bodywork. The use of covers to conceal the rear wheel hubs was unusual outside London. While the outline of the attractive AEC grille remained unchanged throughout the Regent V's life, there were differences in the actual finish of the grille – this 1957 bus has vertical slats where later buses had a fine mesh. Royston Morgan

and the first of London's Routemasters – but even these only raise the AEC double-deck average at this time to around 340 a year.

The 30ft-long Bridgemaster was AEC's first attempt at building a low-height model. Developed by Crossley, a sister company in the Associated Commercial Vehicles group, the Bridgemaster was designed as an integral vehicle which was built by yet another ACV company, Park Royal.

It had been introduced in 1956, when manufacturers – if not operators – were keen to explore the advantages of an integrated structure. The Bridgemaster had independent front suspension with coil springs, and used coil springs at the rear too. However production was soon changed to feature rear air suspension. Originally developed with AEC's AV470 engine, production Bridgemasters used the bigger AV590 – both were units used in the Regent V. So too was the manual gearbox – but there was no semi-automatic or pre-selector option.

A Bridgemaster demonstrator, 9JML, did the rounds from late 1956 covering a range of company and municipal fleets including BET-owned AEC users City of Oxford, Maidstone & District and South Wales Transport, as well as the Leyland-oriented Ribble fleet. It was also tried by a number of municipal operators including Birmingham, Rochdale and Glasgow, and by Scottish group company Western SMT, whose fleet included lowbridge Regent IIIs.

AEC Bridgemaster deliveries

AEC demonstrators	6
Baxter, Airdrie	1
Belfast Corporation	1
Cardiff Corporation	6
City of Oxford	23
East Kent	3
East yorkshire	50
Grimsby-Cleethorpes	6
King Alfred, Winchester ...	4
Leicester City Transport	10
Lincoln Corporation	4
Red Rover, Aylesbury	2
Rotherham Corporation	5
Scottish Omnibuses	1*
Sheffield Corporation	7
Smith, Barhead	2
South Wales	22
Southend Corporation	6
Walsall Corporation	1
Western Welsh	20
Total	**180**

* ordered by Baxter, Airdrie

The rear-entrance aluminium-framed Park Royal body was originally of generally similar appearance to bodies being fitted to other chassis, but once series production got under way in 1958 a new, top-heavy-looking body with steel framing was adopted (largely

to satisfy the requirements of BET) which made the ungainly Bridgemaster instantly recognisable.

All Bridgemasters and most Regent Vs had AEC's new-look front, with a bonnet which did not extend the full width of the vehicle, giving the driver a slightly better view of the kerb than was possible on a Leyland. A stylish grille with a polished metal surround was standard, and changed but little between its first appearance in 1955 and the end of Regent V production 13 years later. A minority of fleets – Glasgow was the biggest – specified a cheaper, slatted pressed-metal grille. A few Regent Vs had exposed radiators and this option was specified until 1960 by Doncaster, Huddersfield and Leeds, and also by Nottingham (in 1955–56) and in 1956–57 by BET companies City of Oxford and East Yorkshire.

From 1960 the outline of the leading edge of the front wings on new-look Regent Vs was changed to incorporate rounded corners. The original square-cornered wings had been prone to catching the brushes on automatic bus washes. AEC used its own engines in the Regent V – the AV470 and AV590 – but three municipal fleets, Aberdeen, Glasgow and Rochdale, took Regent Vs with Gardner 6LW engines in 1955–56. A 5LW Regent V was also available, although none were built.

A joint AEC-Park Royal project was to become one of Britain's most famous double-deckers – the London Transport Routemaster.

Above **As an alternative to the standard AEC grille a cheaper option was this design, seen here on a 1955 Liverpool Corporation Regent V with Crossley body, and also specified by Glasgow Corporation for all of its Regent Vs and by Aberdeen Corporation too. Liverpool bought 193 Regent Vs over a five-year period.** Martin Llewellyn

Left **City of Oxford Motor Services standardised on AEC Regents, and was one of a small number of buyers to specify exposed radiators on its Regent Vs. When this one was delivered in 1957, Regents made up the entire double-deck fleet. It had a Weymann Orion body with platform doors, a feature specified by some operators to improve passenger comfort on long journeys.** Frank Mussett

LT was Britain's biggest bus operator with a fleet of 9,000 buses and trolleybuses in 1958. Assuming a replacement cycle of 15 years – which was the industry average – LT would in theory be buying 600 buses a year, most of them double-deckers. So it was an important customer. While Leyland had the vision to look at new types of double-decker, AEC had an important customer to serve in LT.

The first Routemaster prototype was unveiled at the 1954 Commercial Motor Show, although it did not enter service until February 1956. Built to the then maximum length of 27ft it had the radiator mounted under the floor and with its low bonnet line and simple front end was undeniably a marked visual improvement on existing half-cab designs. The Routemaster's good looks were matched by technical sophistication, with the integral aluminium body being used to hold front and rear subframes instead of being mounted on a conventional chassis.

The Routemaster had independent front suspension using coil springs, and was powered by AEC's 9.6-litre engine driving through a four-speed semi-automatic gearbox. Four prototypes were built – two by Park Royal and one each by Weymann and ECW. The Park Royal buses had AEC units; the other two had Leyland engines and chassis units – at this stage LT was considering dividing its orders between AEC and Leyland, as it had done with the RT and RTL/RTW models. When LT placed an order for 850 Routemasters in 1956 the entire contract went to Park Royal and AEC, and series production started in 1958. By this time the limit

The Bristol Lodekka was bought by state-owned companies throughout Britain. All but one of the Scottish Omnibuses group of companies bought new Lodekkas, all with Gardner engines. A 1956 Western SMT LD6G in Dumfries, one of 20 delivered that year, shows the classic lines of one of Britain's most common buses of the time.
Harry Hay

on overall length was 30ft, and advantage was taken of this to relocate the radiator ahead of the engine, giving the Routemaster its characteristic short snout. Production Routemasters used the AEC AV590 engine, introduced in 1958, although a minority were powered by Leyland's O.600. The first complete production Routemaster, RM8, was at the 1958 Commercial Motor Show.

Both Leyland and AEC had a broad spread of customers for their double-deck models in the late 1950s. Titans were bought by the Scottish Omnibuses group, by BET companies, and by very many municipal fleets. AEC sold to BET and municipal operators. Both manufacturers sold small numbers of new 'deckers to the few independents buying such vehicles.

Of the other manufacturers, Bristol's Lodekka was available exclusively to state-owned operators, with around 350 a year going to companies in the Tilling and Scottish groups. Following on from the two LDX prototypes of 1949–50, series production of the LD model had started in 1954. It was 27ft long and 8ft wide – rather than 26ft long and 7ft 6in wide, the dimensions of the prototypes.

Production Lodekkas also had a rounded new-look front. This usually incorporated a stylised version of Bristol's traditional radiator grille, although a few of the first Lodekkas equipped with Cave-Browne-Cave heating dispensed with this. The grille outline

quickly changed, with a more modern appearance being created during 1955 by raising the lower edge of the moulding. Soon after the front wings were shortened to provide an improved flow of air to the brakes

The Lodekka was offered with a choice of Bristol (LD6B) or Gardner 6LW (LD6G) or 5LW (LD5G) engines and with four- or five-speed constant-mesh gearboxes. The ECW body normally seated 58 or 60. To accommodate the gearbox, which intruded into the saloon, a rearward-facing five-passenger bench seat was placed against the front bulkhead. This, incidentally, was a seating arrangement also used by a number of municipal fleets because it provided one extra seat in the lower saloon.

Daimlers were still selling mainly to municipals, and the average of 200 deliveries a year in the late 1950s masks a high of 316 in 1957 (boosted by substantial deliveries to Glasgow, Manchester and Dundee) and a low of 127 in 1958. Up to the late 1950s Daimler's CV models had a preselector gearbox, but from 1957 they were offered with a four-speed Daimatic semi-automatic gearbox. From 1958 a four-speed David Brown synchromesh gearbox was offered as an option in the CS-series (S for synchromesh) range. There were problems with the synchromesh on the David Brown gearbox and only 40 CS-series chassis were built.

Chassis suitable for 30ft-long bodywork

were introduced by Daimler in 1956. These were identified by a /30 suffix and could be powered by either the Gardner 6LW or, from 1958, the new and bigger 10.45-litre 6LX which offered 150bhp against the 8.4-litre 6LW's 112bhp. Daimler's 10.6-litre CD650 and turbocharged 8.6-litre CD6 were also available, but only four 30ft-long chassis were sold with Daimler engines – to Glasgow Corporation, PMT and to Doncaster independents Rossie Motors and Leon Motor Services. A CSG6/30 chassis was exhibited at the 1958 Commercial Motor Show but was rebuilt to CVG6/30 specification and sold to Walsall Corporation, entering service in 1961 with a forward-entrance Metro-Cammell body.

Guy, like Daimler, tended to be a municipal choice, although two of the country's largest independents – Lancashire United and West Riding – were Arab buyers, as were BET companies East Kent and Northern General. The late 1950s average was 120 Arabs a year for British buyers – but the figure was falling and in the 1960s Arab sales in the home market were never higher than 81 in any one year. Sales of Arab double-deckers to the Scottish Omnibuses group came to an end in 1956 (the last were for Western SMT). The last Arabs for a BET company went to East Kent in 1957, which left Guy dependant on municipal and independent buyers. Most Arab double-deckers had Gardner 5LW or 6LW engines and constant-mesh gearboxes.

Right Daimlers were built in Coventry and made up the bulk of the city's bus fleet. Metro-Cammell bodywork, generally similar to that supplied to Birmingham City Transport, was fitted to 40 Daimler-powered CVD6s delivered in 1952, some of which ran for 20 years. All subsequent Coventry Daimlers had Gardner engines. *Chris Aston*

Below Among the small band of municipal Guy users was South Shields, which ran Arabs with Roe bodywork. South Shields bought Arabs until 1959, then switched to Daimlers, but still bodied by Roe. This is a 1955 Arab IV from a batch of six which were the undertaking's first buses with new-look fronts. *Chris Aston*

Daimler and Guy, incidentally, used the same new-look front for their double-deck chassis. This was a stylish design which had been pioneered by Birmingham City Transport in 1950 (where it was also fitted to Crossleys). It was superseded on Daimlers in 1957 with a rather plainer glass-fibre design, which became known as the Manchester front after its first user. The main advantage of this was that it was an easily detachable one-piece moulding which could be removed much more quickly than the pressed-metal Birmingham design.

The initial Manchester front had parallel vertical sides, but for 30ft-long chassis, which had a wider front frame, Daimler introduced a similar but wider grille assembly which was broader at the bottom than the top. This was fitted to all but the first two 30ft Daimlers (which had Birmingham-style fronts) – with the only other exception being a bus for A1 of Ardrossan fitted with Southdown-style fully-fronted Northern Counties bodywork.

When Daimler adopted the Birmingham new-look front it had quickly stopped offering exposed radiator models; the last exposed-radiator Daimlers entered service with Northampton Corporation towards the end of 1953. Guy, on the other hand, produced

exposed-radiator Arab IVs in small numbers until 1960. The last went to Exeter.

In 1959 Guy, too, opted for a new bonnet and grille. Theirs was rather more stylish than that used by Daimler and was named after a more exotic first customer: Johannesburg. It did not appear on home market Arabs until 1961. However from 1962 and the launch of the revised Arab V, Guy reverted to the Birmingham-style bonnet. Only 25 Arabs with Johannesburg-style fronts entered service in Britain. The operators were the municipal fleets of Blackburn (the biggest user with 12), Burton, Chester and Pontypridd, plus independents Moore of Kelvedon, Morgan of Doncaster, Rees & Williams in Wales and Graham's of Paisley.

And, finally, there was Dennis with the Loline. Total Loline sales over ten years were below 300 – less than one year's output of Titans, Regents or Lodekkas. The Loline was a Lodekka built under licence by Dennis, bringing the Lodekka's benefits to operators outside the nationalised Tilling and

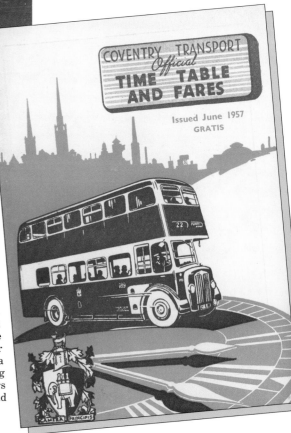

This style of new-look front was fitted to all new Birmingham Corporation double-deckers, starting in 1950 and finishing with the end of the fleet's big postwar bus intake in 1954. It was applied to Crossleys, Guys and Daimlers – but despite being outwardly similar was not transferable between different makes of chassis. It is seen on a 1950 Crossley DD42 with Crossley bodywork to Birmingham designs. Birmingham was the only operator to receive DD42s with new-look fronts. The bus behind is a 1953 Metro-Cammell-bodied **Guy Arab IV.** Malcolm Keeley

Above **On 30ft-long Daimlers the chassis frame was wider at the front and the Manchester-style bonnet was modified to fit. The chassis of this bus operated by Leon of Doncaster was an exhibit at the 1956 Commercial Motor Show, at which time it had an exposed radiator of the type used on the short-lived CD650 chassis. It was sold to Leon in 1961 and fitted with a Roe body. The power unit was Daimler's rare 10.6-litre engine.**
Martin Llewellyn

Below **Arab IVs were built with exposed radiators until 1960, with the last being a batch of five for Exeter Corporation, after which Exeter switched its allegiance to Leyland. Massey built the body. Exeter's bus operations were taken over by NBC in 1970.** Gerald Mead

Scottish groups, even if relatively few of them chose to take advantage of the opportunity. The biggest user would be Dennis's local operator, BET subsidiary Aldershot & District. The Loline's Bristol ancestry was most obvious in the use of a Lodekka-style bonnet, transformed by the fitment of a grille which was a stylised version of the traditional Dennis radiator. Indeed, early advertising for the Loline incorporated a re-touched illustration of a standard Lodekka with ECW body.

The Loline was launched at the 1956 Commercial Motor Show with a Gardner 6LW engine and a choice of Dennis four- or five-speed manual gearboxes. It was designed for 30ft-long bodywork. The first Loline entered service in 1957 with Blue Bus of Willington.

In making purchasing decisions some operators pursued standardisation; others were persuaded by price. Price was often the deciding factor in municipal orders, with some authorities being committed to accepting the lowest tender submitted. In 1957 a double-deck chassis typically cost around £2,300 and a body was about £2,500. Tender prices published by Brighton Corporation showed that for the supply of 20 new buses Leyland was the cheapest (£2,088) and Dennis the most expensive – and by quite a margin – at £2,678. In between came AEC (£2,182), Guy (£2,262) and Daimler (£2,352). Four body-builders submitted tenders. The cheapest was Weymann at £2,330, followed by Park Royal (£2,567), Burlingham (£2,695) and Willowbrook (£2,700).

Brighton bought the cheapest combination, but few would argue that its Weymann-bodied Titans were not a good buy. Incidentally, against a total price of just over £4,400 for Brighton's new motorbuses, further along the south coast new trolleybuses for Bournemouth were costing almost £7,100.

Above right **The Loline was a Bristol Lodekka built under licence by Dennis Bros of Guildford, and the bonnet was recognisably that used on the Lodekka but with a stylised Dennis grille. Only a few were bought by independents, and these included Hutchings & Cornelius of South Petherton. East Lancs built the body. The use of light-coloured wings on a front-engined bus was unusual. Most operators chose a dark colour to help hide any oil and grease marks left by mechanics working on the engine.** Martin Llewellyn

Right **The British Transport Commission had an interest in bus services in Sheffield, Halifax and Huddersfield through joint omnibus committees. This link saw Sheffield receiving the only new Leyland Titans to be bodied by ECW in the 1950s in the shape of five PD2/20 delivered in 1957 which had bodies broadly similar to those fitted to the last Bristol KSWs being built at the same time.** Martin Llewellyn

1958-59

TRAVELLIN' LIGHT

IN 1958 British bus operators took delivery of 1,810 new double-deckers. Over half of these – 926 – were Titans, as Leyland's double-deck market share peaked at just over 50 per cent. Next came 365 Bristol Lodekkas, followed by 157 AEC Regents and 127 Daimler CV-series. All other manufacturers delivered fewer than 100 vehicles. And Leyland's Atlantean? There were just four, including a demonstrator.

The importance of the double-decker in British urban transport can be seen in the fact that out of 18,900 buses in municipal service in 1958, 17,700 – that's 94 per cent – were double-deckers.

Leyland's Titan was being bought by fleets throughout the country. Glasgow Corporation took over 100 PD2s in 1958 alone, as part of an order for 300 to replace tramcars in the city. They had 61-seat rear-entrance Alexander bodies and Pneumocyclic gearboxes. Leeds,

too, was buying Titans to replace trams – showing that Leyland's advertising slogan of 30 years earlier – "Buy a Titan and bury a tram" – still held good. Leeds opted for 71 high-capacity PD3s, with 70-seat rear-entrance Roe bodywork. Like Glasgow, Leeds specified Leyland's Pneumocyclic gearbox.

Other major deliveries which helped boost Leyland's 1958 figures included 98 Titans to Manchester, 44 to Oldham, and 132 to BET group companies.

In the big municipal fleets orders were generally split between at least two manufacturers. Glasgow was buying 100 Daimler CVG6s, delivered in 1957–58 and with bodies identical to those on the Titans, and in 1958 also took delivery of its first 30ft-long motorbus, a one-off Daimler CVD650/30 with Alexander body. Glasgow was taking delivery of new BUT trolleybuses too, and the bulk of an order for 90 with double-deck Crossley

bodies entered service in 1958, marking the last big fleet order for Crossley bodywork – as well as the last big British order for trolleybuses.

Trolleybuses were not subject to the same regulations as motorbuses and Glasgow took advantage of this to convert one tram route to 50-seat single-deck trolleybuses which were 35ft long when the legal maximum for a motorbus was still 30ft. The intention was

In 1958 Glasgow Corporation obtained Ministry of Transport approval to convert a suburban tram route to trolleybus operation using 35ft-long BUT single-deckers, at a time when the maximum length limit was still 30ft. These were intended to be used as 70-passenger buses and can be seen as the forerunners of the high-capacity single-deckers which would replace half-cab double-deckers in many British towns and cities in the mid-1960s. Chris Aston

that they would carry up to 20 standing passengers but opposition from the Transport & General Workers Union – something which comes up again in this story – saw that figure reduced to eight. Glasgow's long single-deckers were BUTs with Burlingham bodies.

In Leeds the PD3 Titans were being delivered at the same time as 15 short AEC Regent Vs, which followed Regent deliveries totalling 135 in 1956–57. They would be followed in 1959 by 30 Daimler CVG6LX/30s as Leeds moved decisively to maximum capacity buses. All of this was good business for Roe, whose factory was at Crossgates in the east of the city. Leeds was Roe's biggest customer and in the late 1950s was buying an average of 60 bodies a year from its local builder, representing almost one-third of the company's output.

Sheffield, like Leeds, divided its chassis business and in 1958 it was taking PD2s with bodies by Roe and Weymann, following on from AEC Regents in the mid-1950s and accompanied by six AEC Bridgemasters, the first 30ft 'deckers in the fleet. Here, too, there was a move to big buses and from 1959 all new vehicles were 30ft long. The Bridgemasters at Sheffield carried a substantial price premium, reportedly costing £5,926 each against a quote of £2,440 for a Regent V chassis and £2,595 for an Alexander body to fit it – a total of £5,035.

Across the Pennines, Manchester Corporation stayed with shorter models. It took 150 PD2s in 1958–59, marking a switch from Daimler who had been the key supplier in the middle of the decade. Manchester squeezed 65 seats into the bodies on its PD2s which were supplied by Metro-Cammell (100) and Burlingham (50). Manchester went for a conservative specification with exposed radiators, synchromesh gearboxes and vacuum brakes, although six of the Burlingham-bodied Titans had Pneumocyclic gearboxes and air brakes, the latter feature an option on the PD2 since 1953.

Nearby Oldham Corporation bought its biggest single batch of Titans, 44, in 1958 to replace its last pre-war buses, also Titans. These were to a similar mechanical specification to Manchester's, but with new-look fronts. Bodies for the Oldham PD2s were supplied by three builders – Metro-Cammell, Northern Counties and Roe. From 1952 to 1964 all new double-deck buses for Oldham were Leyland Titans. The purchase of so many new buses in a short space of time – 44 buses equalled 20 per cent of the Oldham fleet – did in fact store up problems for the future. All would require routine recertification after seven years, putting pressure on Oldham's maintenance facilities which in 1965–66 led to it buying 16 elderly PD2s from Bolton, Halifax and Sheffield corporations and hiring in another 40 buses – mainly Titans – from a number of municipal fleets in Lancashire and Yorkshire.

BET would become a major buyer of Atlanteans in the model's first few years, but in 1958 PD3s were being delivered to a number of its companies. BET had embraced the high-capacity PD3 with enthusiasm and in 1957 had taken over 100. The biggest buyer of these – with 70 – was Ribble, while PMT took 16 and Southdown got an initial batch of 15.

Southdown's PD3s had fully-fronted Northern Counties bodies of a rather old-fashioned appearance with their shallow windscreens and a short bay in mid-wheelbase to achieve the 30ft length. These were the first forward-entrance double-deck bodies to be built by Northern Counties. Ribble had its PD3s bodied locally by Burlingham – marking the Blackpool coachbuilder's biggest single 1950s bus order. The full-width cabs on the buses for Southdown and Ribble eliminated the glazed bulkhead behind the engine, giving

Southdown specified Northern Counties bodies with full-width cabs on its first PD3s in 1957 and this became the fleet standard until 1967, by which time the company was operating 285 broadly similar vehicles. The short bay in the centre was a feature of highbridge Northern Counties bodies on most (but not all) PD3s, but not on other 30ft-long chassis. The body style for Southdown changed little over the years. This 1965 bus has twin headlights, a feature adopted in 1964.
Royston Morgan

the driver a clearer view of the platform and the doors – but increasing interior noise levels.

Ribble, incidentally, chose a single-piece air-operated sliding door, while Southdown went for a four-leaf double jack-knife arrangement – which in the end proved the more popular style of door for forward-entrance bodies. Jack-knife doors were quicker to open and with four relatively light leaves rather than one single heavy door required less robust operating mechanisms.

Above **Ribble, like Southdown, specified full-fronts on the bodywork for its PD3s. The first, as seen here, were built by Burlingham, while later Titans had Metro-Cammell bodies. Ribble was unusual in using a sliding platform door. Most forward-entrance buses had double jack-knife doors. Only one fully-fronted Burlingham body of this style was built for an operator other than Ribble – on a Guy Arab IV for Wolverhampton Corporation.** David Brown

Left **Not all operators wanted maximum-capacity double-deckers. Leyland Titans were the standard West Monmouthshire Omnibus Board double-decker from 1953 to 1966, after which new bus purchases switched to Leopard single-deckers. This is a 1958 PD2/40 with Willowbrook body which, as on all postwar West Mon double-deckers, was of lowbridge layout.** Gerald Mead

PMT's first PD3 Titan had been an exhibit at the 1956 Commercial Motor Show and had a unique six-bay Metro-Cammell Orion body. All subsequent 30ft-long Orions had five-bay bodywork, even though a drawing of the six-bay version featured in MCW's brochures until at least 1962. The remaining 15 PD3s for PMT had forward-entrance Aurora-style bodies by Metro-Cammell.

In 1958 Northern General and its associates between them took 55 PD3s, Ribble had a further 35, Trent took 22 and Southdown had 15 more. The buses for fleets in the north-east and for Trent were of conventional rear-entrance layout with bodywork by Metro-Cammell, Burlingham (for Sunderland District) and Willowbrook (for Trent). The Ribble and Southdown buses were similar to those delivered in 1957.

The BET fleets which were not taking PD3s were generally buying 30ft-long Regent Vs – for example East Kent, South Wales Transport and Yorkshire Woollen. East Kent took 40 in 1959 with handsome fully-fronted Park Royal bodies, and the 30ft Regent V became the company's standard double-decker until 1967 by which time it was running 161.

Unusual among the Regent Vs delivered to SWT in 1959 were two with 37-seat single-deck bodywork by Roe for operation on a route serving Llanelly dock. Six similar buses followed in 1963 and were the last new half-cab single-deckers built for operation in Britain. The relatively low chassis frame of the Regent V when compared with the mid-engined Reliance (SWT's normal choice for single-deck bus work) lowered the overall body height to just 8ft 10in to give sufficient clearance for operation under low railway bridges in the docks area.

One BET company, Aldershot & District, supported local industry by buying Dennis Lolines. It took 34 in 1958 with Gardner engines and 68-seat East Lancs rear-entrance bodies. Like all other BET deliveries in that year they were 30ft long. This was the last year in which BET would take delivery of rear-entrance buses; from 1959 all new double-deckers were of front- or forward-entrance layout – excepting those for Midland Red, which was ironic since Midland Red had been a major user of forward-entrance double-deckers in the late 1930s, the last few of which were still in service.

AURORA
Front Entrance
DOUBLE DECK OMNIBUS BODY
METROPOLITAN·CAMMELL·WEYMANN

This bridge at Llanelly was too low for an underfloor-engined single-decker to squeeze through, so South Wales Transport bought AEC Regent V double-deck chassis and had them fitted with 37-seat single-deck bodies by Roe. There were eight in all and those delivered in 1963 were the last new half-cab single-deckers to enter service in Britain.
Chris Aston

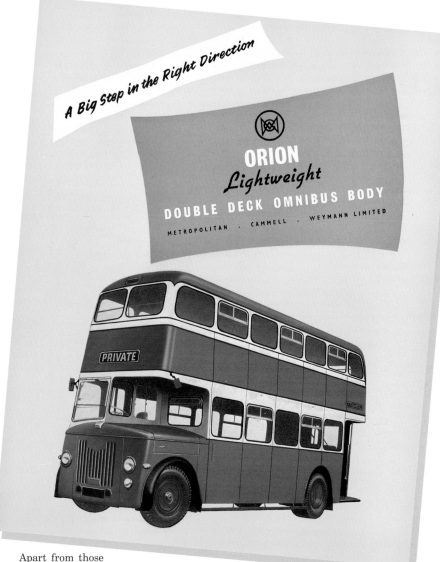

ORION
Lightweight
DOUBLE DECK OMNIBUS BODY
METROPOLITAN · CAMMELL · WEYMANN LIMITED

Apart from those for Aldershot & District, the only other Lolines to enter service in 1958 did so with Leigh and Middlesbrough corporations, Blue Bus of Willington and Hutchings & Cornelius of South Petherton – each of these four operators taking one apiece. Blue Bus had a busy route which passed under a low bridge in Willington; it had previously bought Daimlers with lowbridge bodies.

Daimler sales were dropping rapidly. Deliveries in 1958 were around half the average of the preceding few years with the only big deliveries being 50 to local municipal fleet Coventry, the balance of Glasgow's order for 100, and 18 to West Bromwich. BET subsidiary PMT took a solitary CVD6/30 with forward-entrance Northern Counties body which had been an exhibit at the 1958 Commercial Motor Show. This body (and later Northern Counties bodies on 30ft-long Daimlers) had equal-length bays, dispensing with the short central bay used on bodies being built on PD3 chassis. PMT had bought 30 Daimler CVG5s in 1956, but its 1958 CVD6/30 was to be the last new CV-series Daimler for a BET group company. Its turbocharged Daimler engine was replaced by a Leyland O.600 in 1964.

There was some passing interest in turbocharging engines at this time, in part a reaction to rising fuel bills. The theory, supported by test-bench running at steady speeds, was that turbochargers cut fuel use. The reality in urban traffic proved rather different and turbocharging was soon forgotten. In addition to PMT's CVD6/30, Glasgow received five turbocharged Daimler CVD6s in 1959, while in 1960 South Wales Transport fitted a turbo-charged AV470 engine to one of its 1958 Regent Vs.

The other manufacturer selling double-deckers in small numbers was Guy. It was doing rather better than Dennis (87 Arabs against 38 Lolines) but 87 in a year is less than two a week and has to be seen against Leyland deliveries of almost 80 Titans a month. There were no big Arab deliveries in 1958, but small batches were going to a variety of mainly municipal fleets – such as Aberdare (where they were to be the last double-deckers), Blackburn, Cardiff, Middlesbrough, South Shields and Sunderland. Wolverhampton Corporation's first 30ft-long bus was a solitary Arab IV which had a Ribble-style fully-fronted body by Burlingham.

Middlesbrough's Arabs were particularly old-fashioned – with their exposed radiators and lowbridge Northern Counties bodies they appeared more like buses of the late 1940s than the late 1950s. Middlesbrough's operations were constrained by a low railway bridge in the centre of the town and a solitary Gardner-engined Loline purchased in 1958 spelled the end of Guy as a supplier. The undertaking's next order would go to Dennis, for eight Lolines.

While BET's last Guys entered service in 1957, the last Arabs for a BET-associated operator were four with lowbridge Roe bodies for the tiny County Motors fleet in 1958. County operated just 25 vehicles and was owned jointly by BET and the independent West Riding company: in some years it followed West Riding's vehicle policy and in others BET's.

The Scottish Omnibuses group was quick to take advantage of the PD3's extra capacity and in 1958 W Alexander & Sons took 37, while 55 were delivered to Western SMT. All had 67-seat lowbridge bodies by Alexander and Northern Counties. For use on long-distance services some of those operated by Western SMT had platform doors. The Scottish group at this time divided its double-deck orders between the Titan and the Bristol Lodekka.

The Lodekka was, of course, the standard Tilling group bus – with standard perhaps being the operative word. Life must have been relatively straightforward at both Bristol Commercial Vehicles and ECW in 1958. Between them they delivered 365 Lodekkas, all LD models with rear-entrance bodywork. The only major chassis option was a choice of engine – Gardner 6LW, Bristol BVW or, generally for East Anglian fleets, Gardner 5LW. The 8.9-litre BVW was an improved version of the earlier 8.2-litre AVW and had been introduced in 1957.

Body variations were primarily the seating capacity (most were 60-seaters) and the optional fitment of platform doors. This was usually a manually-operated two-piece door which, to meet Construction & Use Regulations, necessitated the fitment of an emergency door on the rear of the platform. A few operators specified Cave-Browne-Cave heating, identifiable by the radiators which flanked the destination display.

Unlike BET, the Tilling group had not

rushed to adopt bigger buses. This reflected the rather different nature of the Tilling companies' operations which – with the notable exception of the city of Bristol – generally served the more rural parts of England and Wales. In 1957 Bristol had built half-a-dozen 30ft-long Lodekkas, type LDL6G, and a seventh – a prototype for the new F-series range – followed in 1958. It would be 1960 before 30ft-long Lodekkas appeared in any quantity, with the introduction of the popular FLF-series. The LDL offered 70 seats, 10 more than on a standard LD.

Right **Guy Arab sales to BET companies ceased in 1957. Among Arab buyers in the mid-1950s was Northern General. Its last were delivered in 1956 and like all Northern General half-cabs – until the arrival of the Routemasters in 1964 – had exposed radiators. There were 20 in the batch and they had 63-seat Park Royal bodies. Many urban operators were cutting back on the display of route information in the 1960s, as demonstrated by the over-painting of the destination box above the platform. The Northern General Guys were withdrawn in 1969.** Chris Aston

Below **The classic LD-series Lodekka was phased out of production in 1960–61. It was an attractively-proportioned bus, as demonstrated by a 1956 Eastern National LD6B. The Lodekka's unusual driving position can be seen clearly. At this time most buses had steering wheels which were much closer to the horizontal.** Gerald Mead

Above **While interest in forward entrances on double-deckers in the late 1950s was fuelled by the move to high-capacity 30ft-long models, the concept was far from new. It had been popular with a number of operators in the 1930s, but after World War 2 it was only Barton Transport of Nottingham which showed any substantial continuing interest. Barton took batches of Leyland Titan PD1s with lowbridge Duple bodies which featured ornate mouldings.** Geoff Lumb

Below **Skills of Nottingham operated a small number of double-deckers bought new. The last were two Leyland Titan PD3s with Metro-Cammell bodies – an unusual choice for a small operator – which entered service in 1959. The forward-entrance body relieved the conductor of the responsibility of keeping an eye on passengers on the platform, giving him (or her) more time to concentrate on collecting fares.** Geoff Lumb

The increased length limit had rekindled interest in forward-entrance double-deckers. The concept wasn't new – it had been popular with several Midlands operators in the 1930s, and was used by Barton Transport in 1947–48 and by Birch Bros around the same time. This renewed interest was primarily the result of concerns that adding an extra 10 passengers would make it more difficult for the conductor to collect fares and keep an eye on the platform. By moving the entrance to the front, the platform area and the doors could be under the driver's control.

This ultimately did away with the need for the conductor to use the bell to indicate that the platform was clear and the bus could move off – the old rule had been one ring of the bell to stop at the next stop, two bells to start and three bells for a full load so that the driver wouldn't stop to pick up any more passengers.

Some places spelt out the new rules. Leeds City Transport, for example, instructed in its rule book that: "The driver need not wait for the bell signal from the conductor to start. When he is satisfied that all is clear he can close the doors and proceed." To this it added a proviso that at known busy stops where there was a risk of overloading the conductor had to be on the platform. "At such places the conductor must indicate to the driver when the doors are to be closed."

MCW promoted its forward-entrance Aurora body by arguing that the conductor could give one-third more time to fare collection then continued: "He is relieved of the responsibility of giving bell signals and supervising the platform, which normally cause much waste of energy and time." Indeed.

Yet not all operators were agreed on the merits of forward entrances and the general manager of Stockton Corporation, W C Wilson, noted: ". . . that passengers accustomed to rear-entrance vehicles do not adjust themselves easily to moving in the opposite direction when boarding and alighting with forward-entrance vehicles." There were also potential operational problems at busy town centre bus stops for fleets running a mix of forward- and rear-entrance buses.

A number of big operators switched to forward entrances as they ordered bigger buses. BET subsidiaries East Kent, Ribble and Southdown have already been mentioned, while among municipal fleets, Bradford, Wigan and Glasgow, for example, switched to forward entrances when they went to the new 30ft limit – although Glasgow already had a fleet of over 150 two- and three-axle 30ft-long rear-entrance trolleybuses.

The Ulster Transport Authority took its first big buses – PD3 Titans – in 1959 and these had fully-fronted forward-entrance bodies which were built by UTA using frames supplied by MCW. When the last entered service in 1963 there were 142 in the fleet.

They were Northern Ireland's last new front-engined double-deckers. Before switching to the PD3, UTA had been rebuilding early postwar Tigers to PD2 specification and the last of these with UTA/MCW Orion bodies entered service in 1958.

While BET companies had in general switched to forward entrances, one large BET operator chose to follow its own distinctive path. Midland Red built its own buses but had on occasion bought double-deckers from outside suppliers. The last, in 1952–53, had been the 100 Leyland Titans with new-look fronts which set the pattern for most new Titans delivered to British operators for the rest of the decade. From 1953 Midland Red added BMMO-built D7s to its fleet. These were 27ft-long chassis of conventional layout with 8-litre BMMO engines and four-speed constant-mesh gearboxes. A total of 350 were built between 1953 and 1957 and were fitted with Metro-Cammell bodies to BMMO designs.

In 1958 BMMO built a prototype of a new 30ft-long 'decker, the D9. The D9 was an innovative machine. It was of integral construction, had rubber suspension (independent at the front), disc brakes and an unusually short wheelbase for a 30ft-long front-engined double-decker – 17ft 11½ in, compared with 18ft 6in for a PD3 Titan. This was the result of having the front axle set back, which meant that access to the cab was

Above **Midland Red built 350 D7 chassis between 1953 and 1957, all of which were bodied by Metro-Cammell to Midland Red's design.** Malcolm Keeley

Below **Midland Red's first 30ft double-decker was the D9, manufactured in-house at the company's** Carlyle Works. The integral D9 was a sophisticated machine with independent front suspension which allowed the 10.5-litre BMMO engine to be mounted lower in the chassis. Series production ran from 1960 to 1966 with a total of 345 D9s being built. Martin Llewellyn

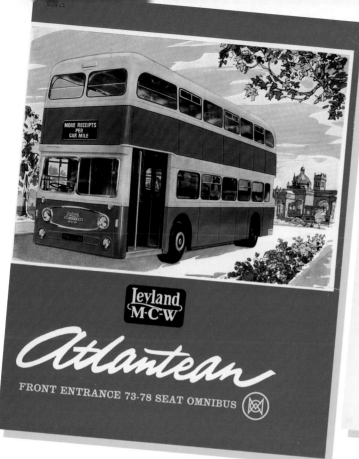

easier, and the turning circle – which is in part a function of the wheelbase – was reduced. The absence of a conventional front axle allowed the new 10.5-litre BMMO engine to be mounted lower in the chassis, which meant a lower bonnet and improved vision for the driver. The D9 also broke new ground for its operator in having a semi-automatic gearbox.

Series production of the D9 at BMMO's Carlyle Works got under way in 1960. The body, also built at Carlyle Works, was of 72-seat rear-entrance layout complete with electrically-operated platform doors and in general appearance was not dissimilar to the bodies supplied by Metro-Cammell for the previous D7 model. And what happened to the D8? That type code, as LD8, was used for the 100 Titans mentioned above. Midland Red's

decision to stick with rear-entrance double-deckers was made on the grounds of faster unloading – the company claimed a 30 per cent advantage over front-entrance types. Interestingly BMMO had in the late 1930s been one of the country's biggest users of forward-entrance double-deckers with its fleet of 335 FEDD (Front Entrance Double Deck) models, the last of which were built in 1939 and survived until 1960.

Three Leyland Atlanteans entered passenger service in 1958, all in December. The operators were Glasgow Corporation, Wallasey Corporation and James of Ammanford – conveniently introducing the model simultaneously to Scotland, England and Wales.

The production Atlantean, launched at the 1958 Commercial Motor Show, differed in a number of respects from the 1956 prototype. For a start, it had a conventional ladder-frame chassis in place of the platform-type used on the prototype. Leyland's publicity material enthused: "Evolution of the Atlantean has been spread over more than four years... its development is a product of engineering ingenuity stimulated by market research. In its new chassis form it has all the virtues associated with the prototype models, but additional benefits as well." What these additional benefits were was not quite clear, as the virtues which the copywriter extolled were

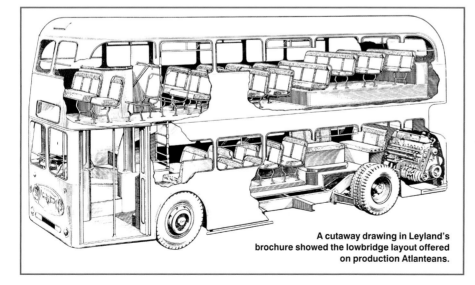

A cutaway drawing in Leyland's brochure showed the lowbridge layout offered on production Atlanteans.

Above The evolution of Massey's basic double-deck design in the 1950s, can be seen when comparing the 1955 Titan PD2/12 on the left with the 1950 Regent III alongside. The basic shape is unchanged, but neater glazing on the Titan sets a style which would change little until the end of Massey production in 1968. Both buses are of lowbridge layout and are in the Southend Corporation fleet. Martin Llewellyn

Below From 1956 to 1963 Maidstone Corporation bought new Massey-bodied Leyland Titans, all with vacuum brakes and manual gearboxes. There were 26 in all. This is a 1956 PD2/20. Harry Hay

precisely those of the prototype – wide doors, the conductor free to collect fares and so on.

In reality, to reduce manufacturing costs (and therefore purchase price) – which was the key aim of the re-design – the Atlantean now had conventional axles and suspension, which meant that it was a full 14ft 6in high when bodied. The independent front suspension used on the prototype had produced unacceptably high tyre wear. And while the body still imparted some strength to the completed vehicle, it was not the semi-integral structure of the MCW-bodied prototype. The new chassis was self-supporting and could therefore be bodied by any builder of metal-framed bodies.

Coded PDR1/1, the new model retained the 125bhp Leyland O.600 engine and Pneumocyclic gearbox as fitted to the prototype. But the engine was now located in a compartment at the rear of the chassis with a solid steel bulkhead between engine and saloon. A single-piece lift-up glass-fibre cover gave access to the engine. On the prototype the engine had been inside the body – as would be seen on ECW-bodied Bristol VRTs from 1968.

At the 1958 Show all three of the above-mentioned operators' Atlanteans were on display, along with one for Maidstone & District. The Wallasey bus had a 78-seat MCW body; Glasgow's had a 78-seat Alexander body, while the James and Maidstone & District vehicles showed that the Atlantean could be bodied to a height of just 13ft 6in by adopting the side-gangway lowbridge-style layout at the rear of the top deck, above that part of the lower saloon where the floor was raised to clear the rear axle. This reduced the carrying capacity to 73.

The body on the Glasgow bus was the first to be completed at Alexander's brand new coachworks in Falkirk which replaced the company's Stirling factory. And while Alexander only ever built conventional full-height Atlanteans, it offered not just one, but two lowbridge versions. The first was similar to the style built by Weymann, with the upper deck gangway running along the nearside at the rear. But the other had two side gangways at the rear with three rows of bench seats on a pedestal in the middle. Alexander claimed it could accommodate 75 people in the former configuration, a figure which was reduced to 71 with twin rear gangways.

Wallasey is generally acknowledged as having been the first operator to put an Atlantean into revenue-earning service, on 8 December 1958. Glasgow's followed on 15 December. The exact date of the James vehicle taking to the road has not been recorded, but it was during December. The Maidstone & District show vehicle did not enter service until January 1959.

Before being delivered to their owners, the Glasgow and James Atlanteans were used for trade press road tests. *Commercial Motor* in mid-October carried a report based on the Glasgow bus, by

respected technical journalist John F Moon. He noted the new model's strong points: "The appeal of the Atlantean is widespread: passengers will appreciate the easy loading, low engine noise and smooth ride; drivers will find it less tiring to handle in all respects; conductors will have reduced responsibilities; maintenance men will welcome the high degree of engine accessibility; and general managers should find that passenger-mile costs are lower."

Another respected journalist, John Dickson-Simpson, tried the James Atlantean for *Bus & Coach*. Like John Moon, he was impressed by its ease of handling and commented on its near ideal weight distribution of 33:67 front to rear when unladen, giving almost the same load to each tyre.

Leyland used the Commercial Motor Show to announce orders for well over 200 Atlanteans for BET subsidiaries Ribble (51), Maidstone & District (50), PMT (45), the Northern General group (32), Trent (22), Devon General (17), East Midland (10) and Yorkshire Traction (10). In addition Sheffield ordered 25, while Manchester signed up for 10. Wallasey's first was part of an order for 30.

As a result, 260 Atlanteans entered service in 1959, out of a total of 1,622 new double-deckers delivered in that year – a 16 per cent market share, which was pretty impressive for such a revolutionary new type. New

Atlanteans were still heavily outnumbered by new Titans, of which there were 483, but the Atlantean outsold all other double-deck models from all other manufacturers, apart from Bristol's Lodekka.

Leyland put four demonstrators on the road and these ran for a variety of operators including the municipal fleets at Bolton, Bury, Caerphilly, Eastbourne, Edinburgh, Great Yarmouth, Plymouth, Preston, Rochdale, Southampton, Southend and Southport, plus BET companies Rhondda and Stratford Blue, and independent Baxter of Airdrie.

The bodies on the early Atlanteans were all designed to take maximum advantage of the 30ft length limit, with upright front and rear profiles. Indeed, to the unpractised eye, there was not a lot to distinguish between the products of MCW, Alexander and, later, Roe bodies, all of which were clearly influenced by BET's requirements.

All had deep windows on the lower deck and shallow ones on the upper deck. They used a steel body structure with pillars extending up to upper deck waist level, on top of which was mounted an aluminium-framed roof section. The use of aluminium and shallow windows helped cut weight – glass is heavy, and so is steel. Weight reduction was important in achieving high carrying capacity and in meeting the Ministry of Transport tilt-test, which required a double-deck bus with a full load on the upper deck to tilt to an angle of 28 degrees without falling over. The Atlantean bodies had, by the standards of the time, a bright and airy lower saloon, but a distinctly claustrophobic upper saloon, with short passengers having to peer out of relatively high-set windows.

The gross vehicle weight limit was 14 tons at this time. If you allowed the regulation 10 stones for each passenger plus the two-man crew – a total of 5 tons 6 cwt on a 78-seater with five standees – that meant a maximum unladen weight of 8 tons 14 cwt, which is pretty close to the figures achieved by early Atlanteans.

All used the same pillar spacing – 3ft 11in – which, incidentally, remained the norm on Alexander bodies on Atlanteans until production ended in 1981. All had flat-glass windscreens, and four-leaf double jack-knife doors. And most operators squeezed in the maximum number of seats – 44 upstairs, 34 down. The lowbridge bodies – all built by Weymann and Metro-Cammell – were generally 72- or 73-seaters with 39 seats in the top deck where the four rearmost rows were four-seat benches on a raised plinth with access from a nearside gangway. The vast majority of lowbridge Atlanteans were for BET companies, although Chesterfield Corporation's first Atlanteans, in 1960, had lowbridge Weymann bodies – the only ones for a municipal fleet.

The October 1959 issue of *Design* magazine, published by the Council of Industrial Design, commented on bus design and of the MCW-bodied Atlantean said: "Only the flush front of this vehicle is pleasing in appearance. From the side and, in particular, the rear the appearance is completely spoilt by the notch effect resulting from the separation of the rear engine from the body."

Design also said more generally that the bus "is one of the most uninspiring vehicles on the road today" and had a tilt at the Routemaster too: "Considering that nothing was taken for granted when it was being designed, this bus is disappointing. To the layman it will probably appear to be little different from its predecessors."

The success of the Atlantean overshadowed another innovative product which was being developed by one of Leyland's smaller rivals – Guy. Guy had come to prominence during World War II with the supply of sturdy Arabs to operators throughout Britain. But its share of the double-deck bus business was not particularly high in the mid 1950s – around 10 per cent in 1955 and 1956, falling to eight per cent in 1957 and to under five per cent in 1958.

Its last big orders in the mid-1950s had included some respected fleets – Southdown had 48 in 1955–56, Edinburgh Corporation took 70 in 1956, East Kent had 25 in 1957 while West Riding bought 45 in the same year, and Lancashire United took 30 in 1958. Three of these fleets then abandoned Guy. Edinburgh turned to Leyland in a big way, and Southdown reverted to Leyland which had long been its main supplier. The third, East Kent, switched to AEC. UK deliveries of Guy Arabs last topped the 100 mark in 1957.

The Gardner-powered Arab was a civilised vehicle, having benefited from a major redesign to meet Birmingham City Transport's requirements, but it was more expensive than a Leyland Titan or an AEC Regent. So Guy came up with a new product which, in the marketing jargon of later years, had a unique selling point: the Wulfrunian. Indeed it had a surfeit of unique selling points – and that proved to be its downfall, as Guy simply did not have the resources to develop such an advanced design. (AEC had turned down the chance to take the concept on after being approached by West Riding, who was to be the main user.)

The Wulfrunian offered most of the advantages of the prototype Atlanteans – 30ft overall length, a relatively low overall height, entrance opposite the driver – and managed to do so without what some conservative operators saw as the Atlantean's weak point, the rear-mounted engine with its attendant complex drive-train. Guy's Atlantean competitor kept the engine at the front, located alongside the driver and offset to the offside to

Above **Ribble, whose territory included the town of Leyland, was perhaps an obvious choice among BET group subsidiaries to get early examples of the Atlantean. Ribble's Atlanteans included examples with lowbridge Weymann bodies, identifiable by their squat appearance and equal-depth windows on both decks. The adoption of the lowbridge layout meant the loss of five seats. A 1960 bus pulls out of Wigan bus station.**
Martin Llewellyn

Below **Most BET companies buying Atlanteans chose conventional highbridge bodywork. A 1959 Trent PDR1 leaves Nottingham's Huntingdon Street bus station in 1963. It has a Metro-Cammell body and like all double-deckers of this period carries a conductor. One-man operation of double-deckers was unthinkable at this time. Note the short window immediately to the rear of the entrance, designed to eliminate a blind spot for the driver.** Iain MacGregor

minimise its intrusion onto the platform area. That this created a cramped driving compartment appears not to have been a major issue at the time.

The engine was Gardner's 6LX, and in the 1950s there were many fleet engineers who favoured Gardner engines because of their legendary economy and longevity. Guy did plan to offer AEC AV590 and Leyland O.600 and O.680 engines too, but none were installed in Wulfrunians. To achieve a low gangway (and thus minimise overall height) Guy used independent front suspension and a drop-centre rear axle. These were, of course, features of the Atlantean prototypes, although Leyland had abandoned them for production chassis.

Guy also fitted disc brakes, at a time when their use on family cars, let alone commercial vehicles, was unheard of. Disc brakes reduced fade and saved weight – and weight, particularly at the front, was clearly a major concern on the Wulfrunian. Cave-Browne-Cave heating was standard. This system (most commonly associated with the Bristol Lodekka) used twin radiators mounted at upper deck floor level. On the Wulfrunian it had the advantage of eliminating a bulky conventional radiator in the already tightly-packed engine area. And, to complete what was a very high specification indeed, Guy fitted air suspension.

A choice of Guy semi-automatic or ZF manual gearboxes was offered, and the gearbox was mounted close to the rear axle – this improved weight distribution and also simplified the gangway layout in the area immediately behind the engine. Another feature influenced by the need to optimise weight distribution was the fuel tank, which was located at the rear.

West Riding was closely involved in the project, its chief engineer being particularly keen on the prospect of reduced brake fade following an incident in which a PD2 Titan was unable to stop after a long descent. The first vehicle, with a steel-framed body built by Roe to Park Royal designs, was exhibited in the demonstration park at the 1959 Scottish Motor Show in November before entering service with West Riding in December. It was a 75-seater and featured a rearward ascending

staircase over the nearside front wheel. The first step was immediately to the right of the entrance door which had narrower leaves on the rear section than on the front so that when the jack-knife doors were open they did not obstruct the staircase.

The Roe body on the first Wulfrunian had an attractive butterfly-style grille which, sadly, was not fitted to production bodies. It also had twin headlights for the first time on a double-deck bus. The overall height was 13ft

Guy Wulfrunian deliveries	
Guy demonstrators	2
Accrington Corporation	2
Bury Corporation	1
County Motors, Lepton	2
Lancashire United	1
West Riding	126
West Wales, Tycroes	1
Wolverhampton Corporation ...	2
Total	**137**

5in and the unladen weight 8 tons 11cwt 2qrs. West Riding placed an initial order for 23.

Back in the real world, among buyers of traditional buses in 1959 Bolton made a move towards forward entrances. It had in 1958 bought its first 30-footers, ten PD3s and seven Daimler CVG6/30s, but these had retained open rear platforms. Its 1959 order was split between six PD2s with rear-entrance Metro-Cammell bodies and five PD3s with

Many fleets standardised on the 30ft maximum length when they switched to forward entrances, although when Bolton took 21 forward-entrance Titans in 1961 they were a mixture of 62-seat PD2s and 73-seat PD3s. The PD3s had East Lancs bodies. An issue which was still being debated was the use of a sliding door for the driver's cab. It had been a feature of London Transport's RT class since the late 1930s, but in many fleets drivers argued that sliding doors were not as effective as hinged doors at keeping out draughts. These were Bolton's last exposed-radiator Titans; the next and final Titan delivery to Bolton would be PD3As with St Helens fronts in 1962. *Chris Aston*

forward-entrance East Lancs bodies. Bolton would buy more short 'deckers, but the 1959 buses were its last with rear entrances.

Bradford, buying its first new double-deckers for six years, went for 30ft-long AEC Regent Vs with 70-seat forward-entrance Metro-Cammell bodies, at a cost of a very precise £5,662 16s 10d each. Fifteen were delivered in 1959 and set the standard for deliveries up to 1964 by which time there would be 120 buses of this type in the city, making up almost one-third of the fleet. However the 100 post-1962 buses had synchromesh instead of semi-automatic gearboxes, following a change of general manager. Wigan, too, switched to 30ft-long forward-entrance buses in 1959, taking ten PD3s with the body order shared between the town's two coachbuilders, Massey and Northern Counties. All subsequent Wigan Titans would be of this layout, although from 1962 it reverted to the shorter PD2 with 64 seats in preference to the 70-seat PD3s. The Northern Counties bodies on Wigan's PD3s retained the short centre bay as first seen on Southdown's PD3s – indeed the body was virtually the same as that supplied to Southdown except that it was of half-cab layout.

Leicester opted for the higher capacity which 30ft-long buses offered, but stayed with rear entrances. Its first PD3s, 12 delivered in 1957, actually replaced high-capacity pre-war three-axle AEC Renowns – the last of the type to be produced and the last still in regular service with their original operator. In 1959 Leicester divided its chassis order between three manufacturers, taking six PD3s, six Daimler CSG6/30s and two AEC Bridgemasters. The Daimlers were to be its last and while AECs would be bought in small numbers, it was the PD3 which would win the bulk of Leicester's business – right through to 1968 by which time there would be 117 in the fleet. A further 20 were on order at that time, but were changed to Atlanteans.

Edinburgh, which had between 1954 and 1957 bought 300 PD2s and 70 Guy Arabs to replace its trams, was taking a break from new bus purchases although it had in 1957 bought

one Leyland PD3 with forward-entrance Alexander body. This was followed by five more in 1959. The 1957 bus had been exhibited at that year's Scottish Motor Show in Glasgow's Kelvin Hall and featured a unique Holmes glass-fibre bonnet and grille assembly – the first sign of Leyland's search for an alternative to the BMMO-style bonnet to give the driver improved kerb vision. Unusually it was chosen to illustrate Leyland's advertising for the PD3 Titan, rather than a more immediately recognisable bus with the established BMMO grille or even an exposed radiator.

In genteel Bournemouth, most of the corporation's buses were of two-door layout, and this was perpetuated on the first 30ft models, ten Weymann-bodied PD3s in 1959 which were the undertaking's first new double-deck motorbuses since 1950. The use of two doors and two staircases reduced the carrying capacity to 62 – the same as most operators would expect in a 27ft-long bus. Ten similar buses followed in 1960, after which Bournemouth moved away from its rear-entrance/front-exit policy. To be correct, the PD3s were Bournemouth's first 30ft-long motorbuses. In 1958–59 it took delivery of 30 Sunbeam MF2B trolleybuses which were also 30ft long and had stylish dual-door Weymann bodies with 63-seats and the forward door located, Atlantean-style, in the front overhang. The last new trolleybuses for service in Britain were nine similar vehicles delivered in 1962.

Part of Bournemouth's gentility had been a fondness for petrol rather than diesel engines for its motorbuses, right up to 1939. A batch of 16 TD5 Titans delivered

in that year were its last petrol-powered double-deckers, though all had been converted to diesel engines by 1956. However petrol-powered double-deckers survived in another resort fleet, Morecambe & Heysham Corporation. These were six 1938 AEC Regents. When they were withdrawn at the end of 1959 they were the last petrol-engined double-deckers in service in Britain.

POETRY IN MOTION

THE 1960 Earls Court show was an interesting one. There were 14 double-deckers from five manufacturers, with bodywork by seven different coachbuilders. Eight were conventional front-engined models, three Wulfrunians, and three were rear-engined. Carrying capacity ranged from 64 (on a Routemaster, the only rear-entrance bus) to 78 on an Atlantean. Unladen weights ranged from 7 tons 5cwt (the Routemaster again), to 8 tons 15cwt 2qrs (the Atlantean again). The most significant newcomer was from Daimler, although it would have been a brave man (or woman) who would have forecast that the new rear-engined Fleetline would reverse Daimler's declining sales. Deliveries of conventional CV-series double-deckers had fallen to an all-time low of just 50 in 1960, from a yearly average of just under 200 in the latter half of the 1950s. From

1963 Daimler would be selling almost 500 double-deckers a year, most of them Fleetlines, although sales of conventional chassis would pick-up too.

The Fleetline took a leaf out of Leyland's book. The chassis layout followed that pioneered by the Atlantean, with a transverse rear engine and space for an entrance in the front overhang. Even the wheelbase was the same, at 16ft 3in. Initially coded RE30 – Rear Engine, 30ft long – the prototype shown at Earls Court had an 8.6-litre Daimler CD6 engine, rated at 125bhp. The CD6 had first been seen in Daimler's wartime CWD6 chassis, and then in the CVD6 which followed it. During the 1950s more and more Daimler operators switched to the Gardner-engined CVG6 and the CD6's popularity

waned with barely two-dozen being delivered between 1955 and 1960.

Daimler wisely announced at the Fleetline's launch that it would be offered with a Gardner engine, and this became the standard power unit. The prototype was fitted with a 6LX before it entered demonstration service – with Birmingham City Transport whose livery it carried – in December 1960.

The Fleetline used Daimler's Daimatic four-speed semi-automatic gearbox and, scoring points over the Atlantean, had a drop-centre rear axle, something which Leyland had abandoned in its search to cut costs and complexity. This meant that the Fleetline could be fitted with 13ft 6in high bodywork without resorting to the strange semi-lowbridge layout needed in the Atlantean.

The show vehicle – which was registered 7000HP – had a 77-seat Weymann body which looked little different from the standard BET-style double-deck body being fitted to Atlanteans apart from having twin headlights and a large Daimler badge on the front. (Most early Atlanteans carried no identification on the front panel, but had a badge on the engine cover which showed Atlas supporting the world.) It weighed 8 tons 7cwt – which was 5cwt less than the lighter of the two Atlanteans on show. Daimler also showed a CD6-engined Fleetline chassis, but this was never bodied. The RE30 chassis designation quickly gave way to CRG6.

Coincidentally, as Daimler was launching its lowheight Fleetline, the last CVG6 with a lowbridge body was entering service with Blue Bus of Willington. The body was by Willowbrook, and was also the last from that builder to feature a sunken side gangway.

The Wulfrunian made its first Earls Court appearance at the 1960 show and did so in strength. There were two with Roe bodies – for West Riding and Bury Corporation – plus one with Northern Counties bodywork for Lancashire United Transport. Guy also exhibited a bare chassis. The Bury bus was a one-off – Bury had been buying Leyland Titans – and it had a short life with its original owner, being sold in 1963. LUT was a fairly regular Guy customer, but here, too, the Wulfrunian was not a success. It lasted little over a year in LUT service, before

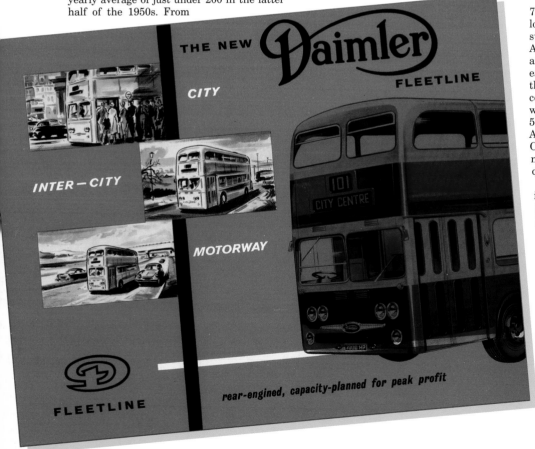

THE NEW *Daimler* FLEETLINE

CITY

INTER-CITY

MOTORWAY

FLEETLINE

rear-engined, capacity-planned for peak profit

being sold to West Riding. It was the only Wulfrunian to be bodied by Northern Counties. LUT had two more Wulfrunians on order. They were cancelled and two Arab IVs delivered in their place.

There were two Atlanteans at the show, one with Metro-Cammell bodywork for Sheffield Corporation and one with Roe body for Trent. There were also three Titans. One was an exposed-radiator PD2 with Weymann Aurora body for Halifax Corporation. The other two were PD3s. A fully-fronted Southdown bus was on show, along with a PD3A for Glasgow Corporation.

The PD3A (and companion PD2A models) featured Leyland's new glass-fibre bonnet assembly – generally known as the St Helens front, in the informal tradition of naming a new-look front after the first user of the type. It had a grille similar in appearance to that fitted to Leyland's Vista-Vue truck cab and featured a sculpted bonnet to give the driver a better view of the kerb. From 1960 it replaced the previous BMMO-inspired new-look front – except in Edinburgh, where the corporation produced its own glass fibre bonnet assembly to the BMMO/Leyland design and fitted it to new Titans until its last in 1966.

Southdown's PD3 had a 69-seat Northern Counties body; Glasgow's PD3A had a 72-seat Alexander body. It was Glasgow's only PD3A; the remainder of that undertaking's order for 140 PD3s had the BMMO-type grille.

Above **Bury Corporation's Wulfrunian was an exhibit at the 1960 Commercial Motor Show, and its Roe body featured rather more attractive styling for the upper deck radiator grilles than was standard. Despite the high profile start to its life, Bury's only Guy double-decker was soon on the move, being withdrawn in 1963. It is seen in Wrexham in 1965 with Wright of Penycae.**
Alan Mortimer

Below **The last new Titans for Scottish group companies were of the new PD3A style and entered service in 1961. They were also the last side-gangway lowbridge buses bought new by a Scottish operator. This is a Western SMT PD3A/3 with 67-seat Alexander bodywork of a style bought only by Scottish operators. Similar buses were delivered to the newly-formed Alexander (Midland) and Alexander (Northern) companies.**
Stewart J Brown

There were three Dennis Lolines at Earls Court – an East Lancs-bodied bus for Luton Corporation, a Willowbrook-bodied example for Walsall, and one with Northern Counties body for Barton Transport. All were Loline IIs, with the chassis frame modified to allow the fitment of forward entrance bodywork. The Loline II chassis had first been exhibited at the 1958 Commercial Motor Show and had rear air suspension and was offered with a choice of four engines – Gardner 6LW and 6LX, AEC AV470 and Leyland O.600

Luton Corporation services had to negotiate a low bridge near the railway station and Luton had been buying Leyland PD2s with lowbridge bodies. The last Luton buses of this layout entered service in 1960 alongside a pair of Lolines which had Leyland engines in the interests of standardisation. The Luton Lolines were unusual in being just 27ft 8in long.

However the Barton Transport vehicle was the one which caught operators' attention. Barton had a problem with a low bridge on the Sawley road out of Long Eaton. Too low even for a 13ft 6in lowbridge bus to pass through, this enterprising company's answer was to build a lowbridge body on a lowheight chassis. Thus the Barton Loline was just 12ft 5in high.

Barton Transport's unique lowheight Loline was one of the most stylish front-engined double-deckers built, as well as being the lowest. It had a Leyland O.600 engine and was originally fitted with Cave-Browne-Cave heating. Geoff Lumb

It was of forward-entrance layout and seated 68. The body was of striking appearance too. While other builders were introducing squared styles for rear-engined chassis, Northern Counties chalked up a first on a British double-decker by fitting curved glass windscreens to both decks of the fully-fronted Barton Loline – incidentally, only Northern Counties and Massey built forward-entrance lowbridge bodies in the 1960s. In terms of British bus design the whole thing was a blind alley – but a very attractive one. It remained unique, in part because the Traffic Commissioners refused Barton's application to run it on the route for which it was intended, arguing that the arched railway bridge was potentially hazardous and in consequence the lowbridge Loline spent much of its time on the company's Nottingham to Derby limited-stop service.

AEC's presence at the show comprised two buses which, as time would prove, were not really mainstream models. One was a London

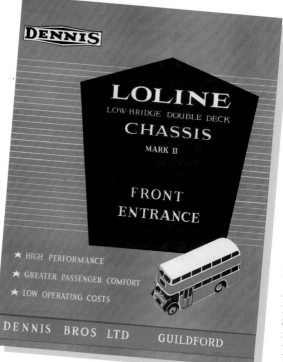

Transport Routemaster. In terms of sales volumes it was a considerable success, but that was down to one customer. That it was the only rear-entrance bus on show can be seen as supporting those who pointed to the concept as being outdated. Yet the Routemaster was a technically sophisticated product, and the swing away from rear entrances was only just beginning to gain momentum.

But the other AEC really was a lost cause: a Bridgemaster. Since its first appearance in 1956 AEC had sold fewer than 90. Only 24 entered service in 1960, including the show bus which was one of 13 delivered to South Wales Transport in 1960–61 and was at Earls Court to show that the Bridgemaster was now available with forward-entrance bodywork. This was made possible by mounting the engine and gearbox at an angle in the chassis and adding a transfer box (which had been a feature of early Bridgemasters). But wouldn't a Regent have been a better bet, and more typical of AEC's success than the Bridgemaster? AEC did have a Regent in the demonstration park, one of 89 ordered by Glasgow Corporation and with an Alexander body similar to that on the Leyland Titan inside the exhibition hall.

The two Glasgow buses were representative of orders totalling 229 forward-entrance double-deckers. The timing of the order – as the move towards rear-engined chassis was just beginning to gain momentum – meant that this was the biggest single order placed for buses of this layout by any British operator. It set Glasgow apart from all of the other big municipal fleets which for bulk orders generally switched straight from front-engined/rear-entrance models to the new-generation Atlantean or Fleetline. They were for the final stage of the city's massive tram replacement programme. At the start of 1960 there were still around 425 trams in Glasgow, some dating back to Edwardian times. Glasgow had, incidentally, intended that its new Regent Vs would have Gardner engines as on its previous batch but AEC claimed that there was insufficient space to accommodate the 6LW and the buses were in the end ordered with AEC AV590 units.

The speculative build of double-deckers for stock by manufacturers or dealers was rare in the 1960s, but at the start of the decade Millburn Motors, the Glasgow-based Leyland dealer, had two Glasgow-style bodies built on PD3 chassis by Alexander. They differed from the Glasgow vehicles only in the interior trim colours, and were finished in grey undercoat. In the spring of 1962 Millburn Motors found buyers for the two – Carmichael of Glenboig (the company's first – and last – new double-decker) and A1 of Ardrossan.

Production of BMMO's interesting D9 got under way in 1960, at the rate of around one

Above **Southend Corporation took six AEC Bridgemasters in 1959-60 with 76-seat rear-entrance Park Royal bodies. They were the last AECs for Southend. Its next lowheight buses, in 1963, would be Leyland Lowlanders.** Harry Hay

Below **In 1957 Liverpool Corporation took delivery of 30 Leyland Titan PD2/30 chassis which were** fitted with Crossley body frames, to be completed by the Corporation at its Edge Hill works. They stood there until 1961, when they were finished by Metro-Cammell. These were the first Liverpool buses to have heaters, and ten operated in this unpainted finish, which was tried by a small number of operators around this time. The grille was of a style unique to Liverpool. Geoff Lumb

Guy put two yellow-liveried Wulfrunian demonstrators on the road in the summer of 1960 and they visited an impressive number of operators around the country. Both were bodied by Roe. Geoff Lumb

bus a week. The disc brakes on the 1958 prototype had not been a resounding success. There were problems with heat dissipation on the rear brakes, and early D9s had disc brakes on the front wheels only. But even this proved unsatisfactory and before long BMMO was fitting conventional drum brakes all round on new D9s – and retrofitting them to the earlier buses too.

With production in full swing at Park Royal, it was another specialised type, the Routemaster, which was Britain's top double-decker in 1960, with 440 being delivered to LT. This put it ahead of the Titan (374), Atlantean (373) and Lodekka (352).

Meanwhile Guy was plugging its revolutionary Wulfrunian. The original West Riding bus was followed in the summer of 1960 by two Roe-bodied demonstrators, 7800DA and

8072DA, whose yellow and black livery had its inspiration in the colours of the Wolverhampton Wanderers football team. The demonstrators travelled widely and were tried by a number of major operators including the municipal fleets in Belfast, Birmingham, Edinburgh, Glasgow, Great Yarmouth, Nottingham, Southampton and Wolverhampton, as well as by BET subsidiaries East Kent and Southdown. Belfast, which had been a Guy customer at the start of the 1950s, actually placed an order for one, but later thought better of this decision and cancelled it. Another municipal fleet to cancel was Rotherham, which had ordered three.

Commercial Motor carried out a road test of one of the Wulfrunian demonstrators in 1960 and published a glowing report. "Its disc brakes make periodic adjustment unnecessary, simplify friction-material changing and give consistent retardation under all conditions. Moreover, it is light and pleasant to drive, and its general standard of passenger comfort has no equal in this country . . . It might be thought that all these major advantages must be accompanied by a certain number of disadvantages. Try as I might,

however, no serious faults became apparent while I was testing the Wulfrunian."

The road tester's words would come back to haunt him.

Fuel consumption on the test – fully laden – ranged from 5.9mpg with six stops per mile to 12.4mpg when running non-stop at an average speed of 27mph. In actual service conditions West Riding's chief engineer, Ron Brooke, claimed a creditable 9 to 9.5mpg. The Wulfrunian demonstrators had relatively short lives and after standing idle at Guy's factory for a few years were sold to West Riding in 1966 where they were broken up for spare parts.

West Riding considered having Wulfrunians bodied as single-deckers and an order for six was announced in 1960. However it thought better of the idea, in part because the intrusion of wheelarches and suspension units would have kept the seating capacity down to about 40.

In 1960 the Atlantean's sales performance was impressive – 373 entered service, out of a total of 1,945 new double-deckers, to give a 20 per cent market share. By this time Routemaster production was in full swing, and new Routemasters – 440 – outnumbered new Atlanteans. But Leyland's high-capacity bus was doing well – although sales were about to take a dip.

Much of the early enthusiasm for the Atlantean came from BET. Of the 637 in service at the end of 1960, over 80 per cent – 517 vehicles – were running for BET companies, which took almost 300 in 1960. Interesting among these were ten for Mexborough & Swinton, which operated 30 trolleybuses and 16 motorbuses in south Yorkshire. They were the company's first double-deckers and they played a part in bringing to an end the last electric operations of the BET group. Mexborough & Swinton's trolleybus system closed in March 1961.

Most of the remaining 120 Atlanteans running in 1960 were with 12 municipal fleets – Birmingham, Chesterfield, Great Yarmouth, Hull, Newcastle, Plymouth, Sheffield and Wallasey plus, with one Atlantean each, Belfast, Glasgow, Liverpool and Walsall. Among those 12 municipalities the arrival of the Atlantean brought to an immediate end the purchase of front-engined buses by four: Hull, Newcastle, Plymouth and Wallasey. Great Yarmouth bought one last batch of front-engined buses – from Daimler – in 1961, while Belfast's last front-engined bus was a Dennis Loline, also in 1961.

Belfast's last significant intake of new buses had been 100 Daimler CVG6s delivered in 1952–53 (accompanied by 100 ex-London wartime Daimlers which were rebodied in 1955–56). It had then bought one AEC Bridgemaster in 1958 (with a locally-built

Hull Corporation's first new double-deck buses for five years were five Atlanteans delivered in 1960. These had Roe bodies. All bodies on early Atlanteans were heavily influenced by the requirements of the BET group and it took a sharp eye to distinguish the products of Roe, Metro-Cammell and Alexander. This is a 1963 bus, at which time Hull was running 49 Atlanteans.
Martin Llewellyn

Harkness body produced on Crossley frames), along with a solitary Sunbeam trolleybus (its last). A fleet replacement programme was clearly imminent when its one Atlantean with Alexander body was taken into stock in 1960.

Birmingham City Transport with over 1,800 buses was Britain's biggest municipal fleet and its 1960 Atlantean was ostensibly a demonstrator, with a Metro-Cammell body in Birmingham livery. It was purchased in 1961, along with a further ten similar buses which no doubt fired Leyland's hopes for bigger orders to follow. Birmingham, like Belfast, had invested heavily in fleet replacement after the war, buying 1,700 buses between 1947 and 1954 which effectively replaced its entire prewar fleet, as well as its trolleybuses and trams – so no new buses were needed for six or seven years. In the second half of the 1950s Birmingham purchased just one bus, a Bridgemaster in 1957.

In Liverpool the solitary Atlantean was one of three vehicles purchased in 1959 for evaluation and given fleet numbers E1–3 with E indicating experimental. The Atlantean was E2. E1 was a 30ft-long AEC Regent V with a fully-fronted Park Royal body of the type being built for East Kent. It was an LD2RA model with AV590 engine, semi-automatic gearbox and air brakes. Liverpool's own Regent Vs were 27ft-long synchromesh D3RV models with A218 engines (the predecessor of the AV590) and vacuum

brakes. E3 was a rear-entrance AEC Bridgemaster which had been an AEC demonstrator and which Liverpool purchased at the knock-down price of £3,657. A new Bridgemaster cost around £6,000.

Liverpool had, incidentally, been impressed by the concept of high-capacity double-deckers and in particular the 33ft 6in-long 106-passenger three-axle Guy Arabs being supplied to Johannesburg Municipal Transport. In a paper presented to the Public Transport Association in 1959 the undertaking's deputy general manager, F H Clayton, argued in favour of 95-seat 36ft-long double-deckers with the top deck open only at peak times. This, he said, would cut the Liverpool fleet from 1,100 to 750 buses. Liverpool proved the practicality of big buses by running a 36ft-long export chassis – presumably borrowed from nearby Leyland – over some of its routes. Wooden planks were fitted to simulate the box dimensions of the body.

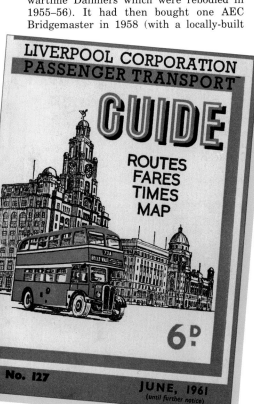

LIVERPOOL CORPORATION
PASSENGER TRANSPORT
GUIDE
ROUTES
FARES
TIMES
MAP
6ᴰ
No. 127
JUNE, 1961
(until further notice)

models, having bodied one of the original Lowloaders and the two Atlantean prototypes. MCW's two factories – Metro-Cammell at Elmdon and Weymann at Addlestone – bodied most of these early Atlanteans. Just over 550 of the PDR1/1s running in 1960 had MCW group bodies. After bodying Glasgow's first in 1958, Alexander did not build any more bodies on Atlanteans until the end of 1959, with deliveries starting in January 1960 of a batch of 17 to companies in the Northern General group. Alexander bodied just three other Atlanteans in 1960 – one each for the municipal fleets in Belfast, Sheffield and Newcastle.

In 1960 a third builder, Roe, started bodying Atlanteans. During that year it supplied 82 to BET group companies – Devon General, Trent and the Northern General group – and the first of an order for 10 to Hull, which carried that fleet's streamlined livery, looking a shade anachronistic on a modern and square-styled bus. Roe was a sister company of Park Royal within the ACV group and the decision to have the Leeds coach-builder body BET's Atlanteans was made partly because Park Royal was busy with Routemasters for London. Roe used a steel-framed structure of Park Royal design. A BET order for 67 Park Royal bodies on Atlanteans for East Midland, PMT, Trent and Western Welsh for delivery in 1959–60 was cancelled and re-allocated to Weymann.

Manchester Corporation, which ran 1,300 buses, put its first ten Atlanteans into service in 1960. They were the last ten buses from an order which had originally called for 110 Titans. The Atlanteans had in fact been delivered at the end of 1959, but immediately became the focus of a union dispute over their higher carrying capacity. This delayed their

Above **In June 1959 Silver Star of Porton Down became the first independent operator of a Leyland Atlantean. It built up a fleet of four with Weymann lowbridge bodywork. This 1960 bus shows the company's use of mouldings to improve the appearance of the otherwise plain-looking body. The mouldings were similar to those used for Standerwick's Gay Hostess Atlantean coaches. Silver Star was taken over by Wilts & Dorset in June 1963.** Martin Llewellyn

Below **The first Scottish independent to buy an Atlantean was Chieftain of Hamilton, which was operating two in 1961 – making it Scotland's biggest Atlantean user for a short time. Metro-Cammell built the 77-seat bodywork. It is seen in East Kilbride.** Iain MacGregor

There were four Atlanteans running for independents – two with Silver Star of Porton Down (the first independent Atlantean operator) and one each with Chieftain of Hamilton and Scout of Preston. Chieftain would buy a second in 1961 (making it very briefly Scotland's biggest Atlantean user) before selling out to Central SMT at the end of that year – giving the conservative Scottish Omnibuses group its first taste of rear-engined bus operation. Scout would build up a fleet of five Atlanteans, including an ex-demonstrator, by the time it was taken over by Ribble in December 1961.

MCW had been closely involved with the development of Leyland's new rear-engined

entry into service for four months. Two had
air suspension which was later replaced by
conventional steel springs.

One of the issues which concerned the
unions was standing passengers, and in 1960
municipal operators agreed nationally to a
maximum of five standees on double-deckers
with between 71 and 78 seats. An odd side-
effect of this was the downseating by Leeds
City Transport of some of its 71-seat 30ft-long
deckers. By removing a seat they could carry
three more standing passengers, upping total
capacity from 76 (71 plus five) to 78 (70 plus
eight).

The BET fleets which weren't buying
Atlanteans or 30ft Titans in 1960 were in the
main buying AEC Regents. These included
City of Oxford, Rhondda, South Wales
Transport and Yorkshire Woollen. All had
forward-entrance bodies and, except in
Oxford, were 30ft long. Oxford's Regents were
to be its last; the company had bought little
else for its double-deck fleet in the previous 30
years. South Wales, which had to contend with
low bridges on some routes, took small
numbers of Bridgemasters, a type also in
operation with nearby Western Welsh.

The only BET fleet buying double-deckers
in 1960 which were not AECs or Leylands was
North Western, with 15 Dennis Loline IIs.
Twelve had Leyland O.600 engines (the
company's last double-deckers had been PD2s
in 1956) while the remaining three had
Gardner 6LX units. They were North
Western's first 30ft double-deckers and all had
East Lancs forward-entrance bodies.

In the municipal sector, Dennis Loline IIs
were being supplied to Middlesbrough
Corporation, which specified fully-fronted
forward-entrance Northern Counties bodies,
as well as to Luton and Walsall corporations.
Middlesbrough's 1960 Lolines were its last
front-engined buses.

Elsewhere in the BET organisation BMMO
was continuing its innovative design work
which had produced the D9 double-decker and
the high-speed C5 coach. In 1960 development
was in progress on an underfloor-engined
double-decker.

The idea had been tried before, by AEC in
1950 with its one-off Regent IV which had a
short life. The Regent IV offered no advantages over a Regent III and indeed had some
disadvantages such as greater weight and a

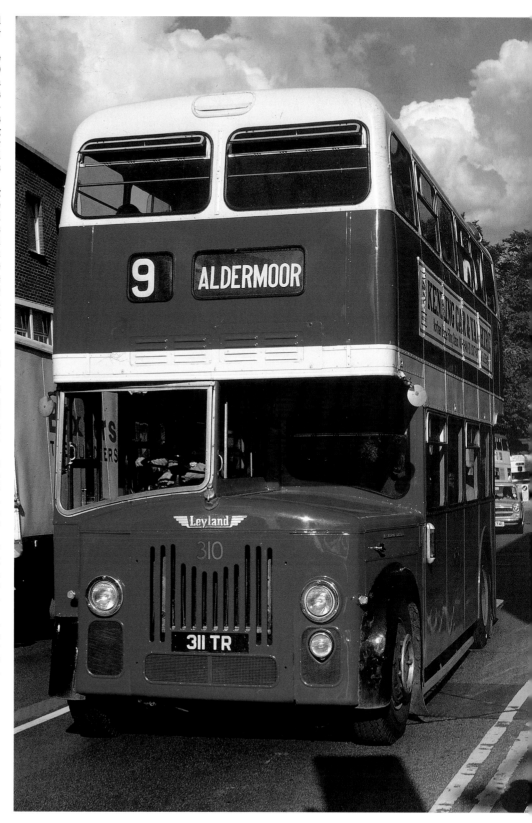

**Park Royal, which had built some of the most
attractive double-deckers of the 1950s, produced a
few incredibly oddly-proportioned vehicles in the
early 1960s. Buyers included Southampton
Corporation with this square-rigged PD2/27 which
entered service in 1961. The 8ft wide body with no
taper at the front emphasises the 7ft 6in-wide
origins of the Leyland new-look front.**
Stewart J Brown

higher floor level. Although it carried two different bodies it never actually entered passenger service and was quietly abandoned.

BMMO's D10 was a different kettle of fish. For a start, it was 30ft long and of integral construction. It also had a set-back front axle, allowing an entrance opposite the driver. An attractive 78-seat BMMO body was built for it, using Metal Sections frames. It had a horizontal version of the 127bhp BMMO 10.5-litre engine which powered the D9. In underfloor-engined single-deckers the engine was located with the cylinder heads facing outwards. For the D10 BMMO reversed this practice so that the flywheel housing, the deepest part of the engine, was located in a position which set it outside that part of the bus where Construction & Use Regulations stipulated a minimum 10in ground clearance. This allowed the engine to be set lower, which in turn reduced the height of the lower deck gangway. The D10's overall height was 14ft 4½ in. To accommodate the engine, the seats on the nearside of the lower deck were raised a few inches, with a step up from the gangway. The floor under the offside seats was at gangway level.

Following the company's experience with the disc-braked D9, plans to use discs all round were abandoned and the D10 had a front disc/rear drum arrangement as on early production D9s. And, again like the D9, it had rubber suspension, independent on the front wheels. The first D10 weighed 8 tons 10cwt 2qrs. This compared with 7 tons 18cwt 2qrs for a D9.

A second D10 in 1961 had two doors – the second being a single-width exit in the rear overhang – and two staircases as well, which reduced the seating capacity to 65. In 1962 the rear door and staircase were removed. The two buses served Midland Red for 12 years.

The Tilling group was sticking with the tried and proven Lodekka. However that model was undergoing improvements and during 1960 production of the original LD was phased out (except for the Scottish group which received its last LDs in 1961) and in its place came the F-series.

The F-series had a modified chassis frame which eliminated the step up from the gangway to the seats in the lower saloon, thus providing a flat floor. Its appearance had in fact been foreshadowed by the Dennis Loline II at the 1958 Earls Court show, and the first of the new F-series Lodekkas at the end of 1959 was a 30ft-long forward-entrance FLF for Bristol Tramways.

The FLF (Flat floor, Long, Forward entrance) would be followed in 1960 by the short FSF, and by the rear-entrance FL and FS models. As with the original Lodekka, bodywork was by ECW and while the body on the rear-entrance F-series models looked little different from that on the LD (although it did

Above **BMMO's first D10 offered 78-seat capacity – six more than in a D9 – by moving the engine under the floor to release the maximum space for passengers. Only two D10s were built.**
Martin Llewellyn

Below **Lodekkas with forward-entrance bodywork had a much more upright front end than had been used on the previous LD range, and the short FSF series, only built between 1960 and 1963, was a** particularly neat design. After 1963 Tilling and Scottish operators had the choice of just two Lodekka models – the short rear-entrance FS and the long forward-entrance FLF. Midland General was one of the few Tilling companies to use a livery other than the standard red or green, and its attractive blue and cream survived until the adoption of a corporate livery by NBC. It took 10 FSF6Gs in 1961-62. Note the fine Mark IV Ford Zodiac behind the bus. Paul Caudell

in fact have side windows which were about five inches longer), the body for the forward-entrance buses had a much more upright front which created more room for upper deck seats ahead of the staircase. It was less traditional, perhaps, but more in keeping with the increasingly square designs which were appearing around this time.

The first FLF had a sliding entrance door, as did the first FSF; but all production FLF and FSF Lodekkas had double jack-knife doors and the original FLF was quickly modified to match. The choice of engines continued unchanged, except that the 94bhp Gardner 5LW was not offered on the 30ft-long F-series models which weighed just over 8 tons unladen. The rear-entrance 30ft-long FL was short-lived. The last was built in 1963 and brought to an end a production run of just 45 vehicles. The biggest user was Red & White Services with 20. Others went to Hants & Dorset, Lincolnshire Road Car, Eastern Counties and Western SMT, which took two.

Hants & Dorset chose FLs because the company was concerned that the FLF with its forward-mounted staircase would restrict visibility for lower-deck passengers and might deter leisure traffic on routes such as those serving the New Forest.

The short forward-entrance model, the FSF, had a short production life too although output did total 218. The last Tilling group FSFs were delivered in 1962. The major users were Brighton Hove & District (15), Bristol Omnibus (38), Crosville (30), United Auto (28) and United Welsh (28). The only Scottish group buyer of the FSF was Central SMT with 48, including the last to be built which were delivered in 1963.

At the end of 1959 Scottish Omnibuses had tested the original Bristol Tramways FLF6B, 995EHW, in service alongside AEC Bridgemaster demonstrator 80WMH. Earlier in the decade Scottish Omnibuses had bought AEC Regent IIIs, but it was the Lodekka, perhaps predictably, which would continue to feature in the company's future orders.

Small numbers of Fleetlines appeared in service in 1961 – eleven to be precise. Ten went to Middlesbrough and one to Scottish independent A1 Service. All had lowheight bodies by Northern Counties to a rather more attractive design than any bodies so far fitted to the Atlantean, a chassis which, incidentally, Northern Counties did not body until 1964. Where the builders on Atlantean chassis had gone for a somewhat utilitarian look, influenced in part by the requirements of BET who was the major buyer of the type, Northern Counties built what was in effect an adaptation of its standard body for front-engined chassis. The A1 bus was at the 1960 Scottish Motor Show.

Northern Counties had taken notice of criticisms of the appearance of the Atlantean's rear profile caused by the distinctive engine pod sitting below the upper saloon floor with an unsightly gap in between. The Wigan bodybuilder's pioneering solution to this aesthetic problem was to develop fairings which filled the gap at either side of the engine while still leaving space for the centre section of the engine cover – which was a separate door on the Fleetline – to be lifted up. From the side, the rear profile was unbroken. All early Northern Counties-bodied Fleetlines had this styling feature and it was an idea other bodybuilders would copy.

It was a slow start for Daimler's new model, which may in part have been caused by engineering the change from a Daimler to a Gardner engine. And it gave no hint of the success which was to come. Demand for Daimler engines had, incidentally, dried up. The last CVD6s were three for Swindon Corporation in 1960. After that just one more Daimler-engined bus entered service, a CVD6/30 with Rossie Motors of Rossington in 1962.

Atlantean deliveries plummeted in 1961 to a low of 188. The revolutionary new bus was not without its problems. While BET's total intake of double-deckers fell by almost 100 vehicles, the number of conventional front-engined buses which that group bought rose by a similar number – which put the squeeze on the Atlantean.

The number of Atlanteans supplied to municipal fleets in 1961 was broadly in line with that in 1960 – around 75 – and most were going to the same buyers too. A notable convert was Newcastle Corporation, which after taking two in 1960, put 25 into service in at the start of 1961. From that point on the Atlantean was Newcastle's standard bus.

All of the BET fleets taking Atlanteans in 1961 were those which already had the type. Ribble, which by 1961 had 100 Atlanteans in service (not counting the 37 Gay Hostess coaches in the Standerwick fleet) switched back to PD3 Titans, a type previously bought in 1957–58. It took 50 PD3s in 1961 and a further 45 in 1962, all with fully-fronted bodies.

This time the bodywork was by Metro-Cammell instead of Burlingham. Burlingham had been taken over by Hendon-based Duple

Scotland's first Fleetline was bought by A1 of Ardrossan, and this 1962 view in A1's Kilmarnock bus station captures the transition which was taking place in many fleets, with a second-hand Roe-bodied Leyland Titan in the background illustrating the old order. The Fleetline had a Northern Counties body and was exhibited at the 1960 Scottish Motor Show before entering service in 1961. Early Fleetlines carried a large Daimler badge with a pattern which echoed the trademark fluted top on traditional Daimler radiators.
Iain MacGregor

Many BET fleets were buying AEC Regent Vs at the start of the 1960s. These were generally 30ft-long and with forward-entrance bodywork, but some fleets also bought 28ft-long models including Rhondda, which added four short Regents to its fleet in 1962. Metro-Cammell built the 65-seat body. John Jones

in 1960 and built its last double-deckers – on BUT trolleybus chassis for Reading Corporation – in 1961. The Duple group already had the facility to build double-deck buses in Loughborough at its Willowbrook subsidiary, and the Burlingham site in Blackpool was about to be renamed Duple (Northern) and devoted exclusively to coach production. In any case, Burlingham was not really a mainstream double-deck builder and it had never been a big supplier of bus bodies to BET. For Ribble Metro-Cammell supplied a fully-fronted version of its 30ft-long Aurora body which gave it a vague resemblance to the Burlingham-bodied PD3s already in operation. Metro-Cammell was already building generally similar bodywork on Guy Arab IVs for Wolverhampton Corporation.

AEC did well out of BET in 1961, although it would be wrong to read this as a reaction against the Atlantean. Many of that year's double-deck deliveries just happened to be to AEC fleets. They included the first Bridgemasters for East Yorkshire, which had Park Royal bodies with a modified upper deck

roof profile to allow safe passage through the Beverley Bar. East Yorkshire took 20 Bridgemasters in 1961, and a further 30 over the following two years. Another newcomer to the Bridgemaster was City of Oxford with ten. Here, too, more would follow in 1962 and 1963. These included the only short (27ft 8in) forward-entrance variants. In fact Bridgemaster deliveries peaked in 1961 – but only at 50.

Two of BET's subsidiaries in South Wales were long-standing AEC users. The only double-deckers bought by Rhondda over a 10-year period from 1956 to 1966 were Regent Vs. South Wales Transport also bought large numbers of Regent Vs every year until 1967. Under BET ownership SWT did not buy any rear-engined double-deckers; it would be well into the NBC era – 1976 – before SWT ordered the type.

As in 1960, so in 1961 the only other supplier of double-deckers to BET alongside Leyland and AEC was Dennis. Aldershot & District, which had bought a batch of Loline Is in 1958, took 20 Loline IIIs in 1961, unusual for an operator this far south in having Alexander bodies. Similar buses were supplied to North Western. These two orders followed Alexander's first delivery of double-deckers to the BET group, on Atlanteans in 1960.

A surprise buyer of Lolines in 1961 was City of Oxford – although they did have AEC engines. Most Lolines were 30ft long; Oxford's

were unusual in being 27ft 6in. They had 63-seat forward-entrance East Lancs bodies – a relatively unusual choice for a BET company – and were to be the fleet's only Lolines.

The Loline III superseded the Mark II in 1961 (Oxford's were the last Mark IIs) and had rear air suspension as standard; it had been an option on the previous model. The Loline III was also available with a Self-Changing Gears epicyclic gearbox and was identifiable by a revised grille of squarer appearance than that used on earlier models. All Loline IIIs had forward-entrance bodywork apart from a pair with East Lancs rear-entrance bodies supplied to Leigh Corporation in 1961.

Guy notched up almost 50 Wulfrunian deliveries in 1961. If this fuelled hopes of some sort of sales breakthrough at the company's Wolverhampton headquarters, they were hopes which would soon be dashed. This was, in fact, the Wulfrunian's best year. The exact number was 47, and 43 of these were for one fleet, West Riding. One went to West Wales of Ammanford (not a regular buyer of new double-deck buses), two to Accrington Corporation and one to Wolverhampton which was buying Arabs at this time.

One unexpected problem with the air suspension on Wulfrunians came not when they were in service, but when they were parked in the depot. As the air pressure dropped and the suspension settled, the buses would lean to one side. However they didn't all necessarily lean in the same direction. The garage staff at West Riding found this out when parked buses started leaning and knocking against each other – no doubt to the unease of the night foreman the first time it happened as the eerie and intermittent banging of stationary buses echoed around the depot in the small hours. The answer was to paint white lines on the depot floor to mark out parking bays which provided enough room for adjacent buses to lean towards each other without touching.

The most unusual Wulfrunians were the pair bought by Accrington, which had rear-entrance East Lancs bodies on chassis with a shortened front overhang. On these the engine was located on the centre-line of the chassis, rather than being offset to the offside. With rear-entrance bodywork there was no need for an offset engine, and this provided more space for the driver. The Accrington buses also had 6LW engines rather than the standard 6LX, and four-speed ZF gearboxes. They were 28ft-long 66-seaters. They only lasted seven years in Accrington and were withdrawn in 1968 – being outlasted by 1951 Titans, which is a pretty strong indictment of the Wulfrunian. Accrington's reason for buying Wulfrunians rather than Arabs appears to have been an announcement by Guy that Arab production was being stopped, although in practice this didn't happen.

Aldershot & District was the biggest user of the Dennis Loline. This is a 1962 Mark III model with 68-seat Alexander bodywork. The advertising panel standing proud of the body was illuminated at night, a feature tried by a number of fleets in the early 1960s but soon abandoned.
Martin Llewellyn

The most unusual Wulfrunians were two supplied to Accrington Corporation which had short front overhangs and rear-entrance East Lancs bodies. They were purchased in 1961, at a time when Guy was indicating that the Arab – a model previously bought by Accrington – was to be discontinued. They were sold in 1968; Arabs delivered in 1959 lasted until 1973.
Alan Mortimer

72/74 seat double-deck bus chassis

Albion Lowlander

5' 8¼" headroom

13' 4¼" overall height unladen

7 CITY CENTRE

LOWLANDER

5' 10¼" headroom

15¼" to step

forward or rear entrance—single-level gangways lower & upper saloons

Leaflet L730

Incidentally, UK sales of the Guy Arab, which had been falling dramatically since the mid-1950s, reached a 1960s high of 81 in 1961. This was due mainly to Blackburn Corporation, which took 12 (and then switched to Leylands), Lancashire United (with 31) and Wolverhampton Corporation with 30 which were all 30ft-long with fully-fronted forward-entrance bodywork by Metro-Cammell.

At the 1961 Scottish Motor Show Leyland launched a new double-decker: the Albion Lowlander. This had a low frame, and was Leyland's response to growing disenchant-ment with the side-gangway lowbridge layout still required by a minority of operators. It also offered competition for the Dennis Loline and AEC Bridgemaster, although with combined annual sales of both these models running at around 100 – say five per cent of the total double-deck market – it hardly seems an area worthy of much attention.

However of greater import were the requirements of the Scottish Omnibuses group. In the late 1950s all Scottish group double-deckers were either lowbridge Titans or lowheight Lodekkas – averaging around 90 of each type every year. The group wanted to stop buying lowbridge buses. Leyland came up with the Lowlander, to be assembled at its Albion factory in Glasgow using kits of parts shipped up from Lancashire.

The Lowlander used the O.600 engine of the PD3 Titan, uprated from 125 to 140bhp. It also used the glass-fibre grille and bonnet assembly of the PD3A but, for Scottish operators at least, with Albion badging. The chassis frame was new, and dropped down behind the front axle. Recognising that high-capacity double-deckers were now increasingly of forward-entrance layout, Leyland designed the Lowlander with a dip in the chassis frame immediately behind the front bulkhead to allow a step-free entrance area. The gearbox – synchromesh or Pneumocyclic – was remote-mounted under the nearside seats (there was a shallow sunken gangway in the lower saloon) – and drive was to a new double-reduction drop-centre rear axle, which would later prove useful in the development of the Atlantean range. Rear air suspension was an option.

Two near-identical sales brochures were produced for operators in Scotland and England, differing only in the use of the Leyland name for those south of the border and the Albion name for those in the north. The Lowlander started off with a healthy order – 106 for the Scottish group – and the first of these, with Alexander body for Western SMT, was exhibited at Kelvin Hall in 1961.

A similar bus, in Glasgow Corporation colours, demonstrated in Glasgow throughout 1962 – which seems just a bit pointless when Glasgow had already committed to buying Atlanteans and had no need for lowheight buses. It was repainted in Edinburgh Corporation colours in 1963 and moved to Scotland's capital on demonstration. Here, too, lowheight buses were not required and the demonstrator was sold to Bamber Bridge Motor Services at the end of the year. Edinburgh did, incidentally, buy one Lowlander. The chassis was delivered to the Corporation's Shrubhill works in 1962 and there it lay gathering dust before being returned to Albion in 1964. It was then sold to Western SMT, entering service in 1965 with a Northern Counties body.

The Lowlander was a bit of a disaster. For a start, Leyland didn't really want to build it. They had in fact tried to convince the conservative Scottish group that the lowbridge Atlantean was the bus they really wanted, reportedly even offering a discount of £150 per chassis to encourage sales. On Leyland's list

Albion Lowlander deliveries

Albion demonstrator	...	...	1
Alexander (Fife)	...	...	7
Alexander (Midland)	...	...	44
Alexander (Northern)	...	...	2
Central SMT	...	...	30
East Midland	...	...	18
Luton Corporation	...	...	16
Ribble	...	...	16
Southend Corporation	...	...	10
South Notts, Gotham	...	...	5
Western SMT	...	...	111 •
Yorkshire Woollen	...	...	14
Total	...	...	**274**

• includes one chassis which had been built for Edinburgh Corporation.

The original Albion Lowlander demonstrator operated first in Glasgow Corporation colours, and was then repainted in Edinburgh's madder and white – it was used for long term evaluation by both fleets. It was then sold to Bamber Bridge Motor Services at the end of 1963. It had an Alexander body and had been an exhibit at the 1961 Scottish Motor Show. In 1967 Bamber Bridge was purchased by Ribble, and this bus then joined Ribble's fleet of Lowlanders. It survived until 1975.
Geoff Lumb

prices of the time this would have brought the Atlantean chassis down to £3,530 – cheaper than the £3,630 listed for an LR1 Lowlander with Pneumocyclic gearbox.

The drop-centre rear axle was a source of problems, and where all of the Scottish group's Titans had unburstable manual gearboxes, the vast majority of Lowlanders had Pneumocyclic gearboxes – a first for that organisation – which could give trouble if subjected to high levels of driver abuse.

And while the chassis was new, the front end was pure PD3A Titan, with its relatively high driving position. The first Alexander-bodied bus could almost have been designed to show just what a compromise the Lowlander was. The front upper deck seats were located higher than the remaining seats, a position dictated by the height of the cab roof. Alexander used what was in effect a lowered version of the body being built on PD3s for Glasgow, and in reducing its height by some 12 inches left room for just a single-line destination and route number display. It would be towards the end of 1962 before any of the Scottish group's Lowlanders entered service. Interestingly there was no weight penalty in switching from the PD3 to the Lowlander. Alexander-bodied examples of both types in the Western SMT fleet weighed around 7 tons 18cwt.

Initially two Lowlander models were listed. The LR1 and LR3 had steel suspension and Pneumocyclic and synchromesh gearboxes respectively. They were soon offered with the option of rear air suspension, becoming the LR5 and LR7. No LR5s were built.

Most bus operators had long considered exterior advertising to be a worthwhile source of added revenue although a small number (such as Salford Corporation) had a policy of not defacing the exteriors of their buses. The early 1960s saw the start of a short-lived interest in fitting illuminated exterior advertisements, generally on the offside of double-deckers.

BET was among the pioneers, and East Kent, North Western and Trent all tried it from 1960. East Kent not only specified illuminated exterior advertising on new buses, but went as far as fitting it to a few existing buses, treating some 12-month-old Regent Vs in 1960. The idea quickly caught on and a sizeable number of buses were delivered in the early 1960s with a back-lit transparent panel on the offside, ready to accept whatever advertising was on offer.

But East Kent's experience was perhaps typical. All of its new double-deckers in 1961–62 had illuminated advertising panels, but from 1963 the company reverted to conventional panelling on the offside and by 1964 it was starting to panel over the illuminated display areas on earlier buses as it became clear that advertisers were not willing to pay enough to cover the added costs involved in providing an illuminated display. The concept was tried by Tilling and Scottish group fleets, by London Transport, and by a number of municipalities – but with no real success.

The rebodying of buses had kept a number of coachbuilders busy in the early part of the 1950s, usually replacing sub-standard wartime bodywork on chassis which still had perhaps ten years' life left in them. But by the start of the 1960s it was relatively uncommon. Three BET operators had Leyland Tigers

Huddersfield Corporation operated high-capacity three-axle trolleybuses and when it was phasing out electric traction in favour of diesel power it ordered 30ft-long double-deckers with 70-seat Roe bodies. A total of 24 Leyland Titan PD3A/2s entered service in the winter of 1961-62 and these would be followed by Daimler CVG6LX/30s. The livery with extensive areas of cream on the front distinguished Corporation-owned motorbuses (which were operating over what had traditionally been trolleybus routes) from those operated by the Huddersfield Joint Omnibus Committee.
Martin Llewellyn

rebodied as "new" double-deckers around this time, reflecting the way in which 35-seat half-cab single-deckers had been rendered obsolete by new 45-seat 30ft-long underfloor-engined models. Rebodying them as double-deckers not only increased their carrying capacity but also helped eliminate old-fashioned single-deck buses.

Yorkshire Traction, which had been rebodying Tigers in the mid-1950s, had new forward-entrance Northern Counties bodies fitted to nine 10-year-old Tigers in 1960–61. They were given new registrations and lasted until 1970–71. A further nine followed in 1963. Yorkshire Woollen had PS2 Tigers rebodied in 1963, sending six to Roe to be fitted with new forward-entrance double-deck bodies. The Yorkshire Woollen buses retained their original registrations.

Yorkshire Traction also carried out rebuilding and rebodying for Stratford Blue on five Tigers in 1961 and 1963. It costed the exercise at £500 for overhauling and rebuilding each chassis plus £3,000 for a new body – a total of £3,500 against £5,000 for a new bus.

An unusual rebodying programme in Doncaster came about as a result of the closure of the town's trolleybus system. The Corporation had between 1955 and 1958 fitted new Roe bodies to wartime trolleybus chassis and, rather than scrap perfectly serviceable bodies as it prepared to scrap its trolleybus system, it instead had them transferred to motorbus chassis. Thus in 1962–63, 20 trolleybus bodies were fitted to 12 new Daimler CVG6s, two new Titan PD2/40s and six 12-year-old PD2/1s whose original Leyland bodies were scrapped.

Gosport & Fareham, which traded as Provincial, had an idiosyncratic vehicle policy. This focused on the use of air-cooled Deutz engines in reconditioned Guy Arab chassis which were fitted with new fully-fronted bodywork by Reading of Portsmouth. The first rebuild was carried out in 1958 and when the last Arab rebuild was completed in 1967 (bringing to an end Reading's role as a double-deck bodybuilder) there were 14 in the fleet.

H Orme White, Provincial's managing director, said that air-cooled engines were lighter (by just 2cwt, it has to be said) and used half as much oil as water-cooled engines. Fuel economy was claimed to average in the region of 9.8mpg, against 9.46 for the company's Gardner 6LWs.

North of the border in 1961 W Alexander & Sons installed Leyland Tiger PS2 running gear – axles, O.600 engines, gearboxes – in new PD3 chassis frames to create 17 of what the company described as PD3/3C chassis. These were fitted with new 67-seat lowbridge Alexander bodies and were re-registered. Aberdeen Corporation had ten 1951 Daimler CVG6s rebodied by Alexander in 1960. Most of these ran until 1971, providing a marginal extension to their operating lives – they ran for 20 years at a time when most Aberdeen buses lasted 18 years.

Preston Corporation didn't go in for rebodying, but did have a programme of rebuilding rear-entrance Leyland-bodied PD2/10 Titans as forward-entrance PD3/6s. This started in 1959 with a Titan which was just five years old – and which was also one of two which were rebuilt from lowbridge to highbridge layout, adding to the complexity of the job. The project was concluded in 1967 by which time eight buses had been rebuilt. All were re-registered, with the later rebuilds having new year-suffix registrations. The

Above **Between 1958 and 1967 Provincial reconditioned 14 Guy Arab chassis which were fitted with Deutz air-cooled engines and new fully-fronted bodies by Reading. This bus was one of**

three rebuilds which used 1946 Guy Arab II chassis which had been new to Yorkshire Woollen. It entered Provincial service in 1963, with a new Hampshire registration. Alan Mortimer

Below **Leyland Tiger PS2 running units were installed in new Titan PD3 chassis frames to produce 17 double-deckers for Alexander at the start of 1961. They had new lowbridge Alexander bodies and all passed to the new Alexander (Midland) company in May 1961. One is seen in Glasgow's Dundas Street bus station.** Harry Hay

longest-lived of the rebuilds was withdrawn in 1979, being a 1961 conversion of a 1952 chassis which suggests Preston got its money's worth from the exercise which had been initiated to provide work for the undertaking's bodyshop at slack periods.

DEVIL IN DISGUISE

IN 1962 Atlantean deliveries picked up again – although at just under 350 not quite reaching 1960 levels. Fleetline deliveries accelerated too, crossing the 100 mark for the first time.

One of the most significant buyers of the Atlantean in the early 1960s was Glasgow Corporation. Glasgow had ordered 150, and the first 90 of these entered service during 1962. This was the first whole-hearted adoption of rear-engined buses by a major municipal fleet. The new buses had stylish Alexander bodies which, taking advantage of a further relaxation in the length limits, were 30ft 8in long, the added length allowing the use of curved glass windscreens on both decks.

Alexander cleverly used the same windscreen for its Atlantean body as was fitted to its new Y-type single-decker, while the Y-type's rear windows were used for the upper deck front of the new Atlantean body. Along with the first Atlanteans came the last of Glasgow's Titans and Regents, bringing an end to half-cab deliveries. The Atlanteans carried Albion badges inset on the Leyland shield in place of the figure of Atlas. Similar Albion badges were fitted to Glasgow's PD3 Titans.

The 78-seat Atlanteans were replacing 56-seat buses delivered in the 1940s, and it was Glasgow's avowed intention to achieve a major reduction in its bus fleet by using fewer, bigger, buses. Glasgow would place repeat Atlantean orders until the end of production, by which time the corporation and the Greater Glasgow PTE which succeeded it would have bought no fewer than 1,448.

The stylish Glasgow Atlanteans caught Leyland's attention and in 1962–63 two were demonstrated to Coventry, Birkenhead and Stockton before Leyland actually bought a two-month-old bus back from Glasgow in the spring of 1963. It was repainted and used as a demonstrator for two years, after which it was sold to Fishwick of Leyland.

The first vehicles from another significant Atlantean order appeared at the end of 1962. Liverpool Corporation had followed Glasgow's lead and ordered 200 Atlanteans, the first two of which were in service by the end of 1962. In fact more had been delivered, but trade union opposition delayed their entry to service until February 1963 when 40 took to the city's streets. Delivery would run through to 1964.

Liverpool, too, decided it wanted something more attractive than the boxy BET-style bodies which had characterised early Atlantean production, and worked with Metro-Cammell to produce a distinctive body with peaks to the front and rear of the roof. The Liverpool Atlanteans also had equal-depth windows on both decks. This was a first on a conventional full-height Atlantean, and was made possible by raising the lower saloon floor level and having a two-step entrance, with the second step located immediately to the rear of the driving compartment. As a consequence the lower edge of the lower saloon windows could be raised a few inches without restricting passengers' outward vision.

Below **Glasgow Corporation and Alexander set new standards for the appearance of rear-engined double-deckers when the first Atlanteans of this style entered service in 1962 to replace the last of the city's trams. Advances in glass fibre moulding made it easy and cheap to produce a sculpted front panel, and other bodybuilders were quick to follow Alexander's lead. Note the badge on the front which incorporated the Albion badge in place of the standard representation of Atlas supporting the world.** Iain MacGregor

Liverpool was also the first operator to fit back-to-back seats over the rear wheelarches in place of inward-facing bench seats for four passengers. To allow this, the chassis of Liverpool's Atlanteans had a non-standard 16ft 9in wheelbase, 6in longer than normal. The steering column was also relocated a few inches to the offside with the aim of improving circulation space in the entrance area.

While the Glasgow Alexander body was the more eye-catching – and far and away the more successful – the Liverpool Metro-Cammell body had some pleasing styling touches, such as a fluted metal strip at skirt level and nicely-shaped first and last side windows. The Liverpool body retained the standard Metro-Cammell flat glass wind-screens, with an eye to minimising replacement costs. While the Glasgow-style Alexander body would find customers throughout Britain (and would be imitated by MCW), the Liverpool body fared less well. The only other buyers were Bolton and Bury corporations.

As in Glasgow, the arrival of the Atlantean in Liverpool meant the end of new half-cabs. The last, 30 Titans, entered service in 1961 and were, incidentally, the first new buses in the fleet to be fitted with heaters, other than experimental vehicles. And Liverpool, like Glasgow (and virtually everywhere else), went for a high seating capacity on its new-generation buses – 76.

At this time the growing use of alternators in preference to generators saw a move from tungsten to fluorescent lighting for bus interiors – in both Glasgow and Liverpool the arrival of the Atlantean heralded a switch to fluorescent interior lights which effectively became standard throughout the bus industry from 1964.

One other thing which Glasgow and Liverpool had in common was the existence of extensive body shops, a relic of tramway days and the in-house manufacture of bodywork for trams. As the tram fleet declined, Glasgow Corporation's Coplawhill works started building Alexander-style bodies on Leyland Titans. The last Coplawhill-built bodies – 26 on PD3 Titans – were indistinguishable from those built by Alexander in Falkirk and were completed in the summer of 1962. Liverpool's Edge Lane works latterly built bodywork using frames supplied by Crossley or Metro-Cammell. The last 30, AEC Regent Vs with Metro-Cammell frames, were built over a two-year period ending in the autumn of 1959. A further 30 Titans delivered in 1957 with Crossley body frames which had been scheduled to be finished at Edge Lane were in fact handed over to Metro-Cammell for completion in 1961.

A surprising Atlantean buyer in 1962 was Salford Corporation. Salford had virtually replaced its entire fleet in a massive new

Above **Liverpool Corporation's order for 200 Atlanteans was at the time the biggest single order placed for the model. Delivery started at the close of 1962 and continued through to the summer of 1964. The 76-seat body by Metro-Cammell was to Liverpool's specification and included an additional step at the entrance to create a level floor in the lower saloon – early Atlanteans had a step up to clear the rear axle. By 1967 Liverpool would be running 380 broadly similar buses.**
Alan Mortimer

Below **It might look like an Alexander body, but this Glasgow Titan has Corporation-built bodywork. The corporation's Coplawhill Works built Alexander-style bodies on 75 PD2s and 25 PD3s between 1958 and 1962. The Albion Titan badge on the front was fitted to Glasgow's PD3s and was not normally seen on PD2s. This bus has the final version of the BMMO-type front with additional cooling grilles.**
Stewart J Brown

vehicle programme between 1947 and 1952 and then bought no new buses for ten years. When new bus deliveries recommenced in 1962 there were 36 Daimler CVG6s – no real surprise there after the purchase of 210 Daimlers a decade earlier – but they were accompanied by two Metro-Cammell-bodied Atlanteans. And in 1963 the orders would in effect be reversed, with Salford buying its first postwar Leyland Titans – 38 PD2s, all with exposed radiators and forward-entrances – and with them a pair of Metro-Cammell-bodied Fleetlines.

The 1962 Fleetline buyers were headed up by Belfast Corporation, which had ordered 88 with bodywork by MH Coachworks. Belfast remained a staunch Fleetline customer – although it did also buy three Atlanteans in 1964–65. MH – the initials of founder Miles Humphries – was a new builder whose roots were in the motor trade. The company recruited the chief body draughtsman of the Ulster Transport Authority, W S Robinson, to come up with designs for the Belfast order. The MH bodies were built on Metal Sections frames. The chassis of Belfast's second Fleetline order – for 63 buses – were shipped to the city in kit form and assembled by MH. MH Coachworks would evolve into Potters (in 1965) which in turn became Alexander (Belfast) in 1969.

Birmingham City Transport, despite having been wooed by Leyland with its Atlantean, took delivery of ten Fleetlines in 1962 to join the 11 Atlanteans already in service. While Leyland had been first off the mark, it was Daimler which won the prize, with an order for 100 Fleetlines for 1963, which was repeated in 1964 and 1965. Birmingham's body orders were divided equally between Metro-Cammell and Park Royal. By 1969, when Birmingham was absorbed by newly-created West Midlands

PTE, it was running 609 Fleetlines (including 24 single-deckers) making it the biggest user of the type at that time, with Fleetlines making up almost half of its fleet.

Manchester Corporation had for most of the 1950s divided its chassis orders between Leyland and Daimler and in 1962 it took 20 Fleetlines, joining the ten Atlanteans purchased in 1960. A further 20 followed in 1963, but were accompanied by 50 front-engined, rear-entrance buses too – 25 PD2 Titans, 20 Daimler CVG6s and five of Daimler's new CCG6 model – illustrative of the uncertainty which remained in some operations about the best way forward.

The Daimler CCG used a Guy constant-mesh gearbox which replaced the unsatisfactory synchromesh 'box of the CSG series – hardly a forward step for drivers, but it followed the acquisition of both Daimler and Guy by the Jaguar group in 1960 and 1961 respectively. This followed Guy having gone into receivership in October 1961. CSG sales had been poor, anyway, totalling a mere 40 between 1959 and 1962.

Guy launched an improved Arab, the MkV, in 1962 with the chassis frame lowered by 2½in to provide a better entrance and floor layout on buses with forward-entrance bodywork where it was possible to have a two-step rather than the normal three-step entrance. A demonstrator with forward-entrance Strachans bodywork, 888DUK, was used to show the Arab V's features. With the Arab V Guy reverted to the Birmingham-style new-look front. The

Strachans body on the demonstrator – which was sold to Harper of Heath Hayes – was unusual in having a peak on the front dome, a feature otherwise found only on bodies on the new generation of rear-engined buses.

Nottingham took delivery of its first rear-engined buses in 1962, and these were Fleetlines. More would follow, but from 1964 Nottingham would be buying Atlanteans too. Other Fleetline buyers in 1962 included Chesterfield, Sheffield and one BET group company, PMT, which had been buying lowbridge Atlanteans – it had 105 – but took one Fleetline with lowheight Northern Counties body. PMT never bought another Atlantean, but did take 50 Fleetlines in the period 1963 to 1965. The first 15 had Northern Counties bodies but the remainder had lowheight Alexander bodies based on the Glasgow Atlantean design but with equal-depth windows on both decks and a two-piece flat-glass windscreen.

The Fleetline effectively killed the lowbridge Atlantean. Almost 320 had been delivered to BET companies between 1959 and 1962. After that the only lowbridge Atlanteans for BET were six delivered to Yorkshire Traction at the start of 1964. Small numbers of lowbridge Atlanteans were delivered to other operators.

Aside from any technical benefits of the Fleetlines, BET also wanted to encourage competition with AEC and Leyland. A high-level meeting between A F R Carling, a director of a number of BET subsidiaries, and Sir William Lyons of Jaguar at the end of 1961 followed Jaguar's purchase of Daimler and Guy. It prompted BET deputy chairman John Spencer Wills to observe that "... it was in the interests of associated companies to encourage competition with Leylands and AEC and,

Top left **The launch of the Fleetline heralded the beginning of the end for Atlanteans with lowbridge bodywork. PMT had 105 lowbridge Atlanteans in its fleet in 1962 when it switched to Fleetlines, initially with Northern Counties bodies. Note the smooth profile to the rear end on this 1963 bus, a design feature pioneered by Northern Counties using valances to fill the space between the engine compartment and the upper deck floor. This was made possible by the use on the Fleetline of a hinged section in the centre of the engine cover.** Iain MacGregor

Centre left **The first Roe-bodied Fleetlines were 15 for Sunderland Corporation with peaked domes front and rear. This body style was unique to Sunderland and, while undeniably distinctive, was perhaps one of the less successful attempts to break away from the boxy look of early rear-engined double-deckers.** Paul Caudell

Left **Guy Arabs with Johannesburg-style bonnets were few and far between. Graham's of Paisley took the only one in Scotland – which was also the last new Guy for a Scottish fleet. It had a Strachans body, marking that company's brief return to double-deck production, and had been an exhibit at the 1962 Commercial Motor Show.** Harry Hay

subject to specifications and other matters being satisfactory, it would be a good thing if companies were to make purchases of Daimler Fleetline vehicles from Jaguars."

A few independents bought Fleetlines in 1962 – A1 took a second; McGill's of Barrhead took their first. Lancashire United, Britain's biggest independent bus company, had seven, and Blue Bus of Willington, an established Daimler user, took a pair. All of these had Northern Counties bodies. LUT split its double-deck order between Fleetlines and Guy Arabs, and would continue to do so until 1965 at which point it temporarily abandoned the Fleetline, buying greater numbers of Arabs to compensate.

It wasn't just the big municipal fleets like Glasgow and Liverpool which took an interest in styling. On the east coast Sunderland Corporation – which ran 178 buses – specified an improved style of body from Roe for its first rear-engined buses, 15 Daimler Fleetlines. Up to this point all Roe bodies on rear-engined chassis had been on Atlanteans for BET companies and for Hull; these were the first Fleetlines to have Roe bodies.

Sunderland took the basic Roe body structure, but had stylish peaks added to the front and rear domes. Mouldings were fitted to the body to suit a bright new livery layout which saw much greater use of cream, making Sunderland's Fleetlines look altogether more attractive than the rather sombre Roe- and Alexander-bodied Atlanteans being run in the area by BET subsidiaries Northern General and Sunderland District. Sunderland specified just 70 seats in its Fleetlines which gave passengers more room and allowed the buses to carry up to eight standees – a total of 78 against the more common 82 or 83 achievable with the maximum of five standees which the unions allowed on a 77- or 78-seat 'decker. It also had the destination display mounted just above the windscreen which meant that the screens could be changed by the driver, rather than by the conductor having to go upstairs to do the job.

The first Sunderland Fleetline was an exhibit at the 1962 Commercial Motor Show, where it vied for attention with an unusual Fleetline for Walsall Corporation. This had no front overhang, which reduced its overall length to 26ft. The driving position was relocated above the front axle and the entrance was immediately behind the front wheel. The body – by Northern Counties – seated 64. It looked good, with its curved front windscreens, but the only advantages it offered over a forward-entrance CVG6 was the removal of the engine from the driving compartment and a tighter turning circle. It was an expensive way of building a 64-seat bus.

There were more conventional Fleetlines on show too, for Manchester Corporation and Lancashire United. There were no front-engined Daimlers at Earls Court, although there was a Roe-bodied CSG6 for South Shields Corporation in the demonstration park.

Inside the hall, the half-cab 'decker was represented by five exhibits. One was a Guy Arab V with Strachans bodywork, in the colours of Graham's Bus Service of Paisley, a company whose fleet was made up mainly of Guys bought both new and second-hand. The 30ft-long Arab was one of the first double-deckers to have been bodied by Strachans for some ten years and had 73 seats. However in this form it failed its tilt test, and when it entered service with Graham's in 1963 it was a 69-seater with four fewer seats in the top deck. It was, incidentally, the last new Guy for a Scottish operator and the only Arab with the Johannesburg-style bonnet to be supplied new to Scotland. It was also the last rear-entrance double-decker to appear at Earls Court.

Guy also exhibited a Wulfrunian (for the last time) but with a bus which was unusual in having the entrance behind the front axle on a chassis with a lengthened wheelbase – 18ft – and a reduced front overhang. It was for Wolverhampton Corporation, and the entrance layout matched that of recently-delivered Arab IVs. The 71-seat body was by East Lancs and the engine was located in the centre-line of the chassis, as on Accrington's two rear-entrance Wulfrunians. It also had drum brakes in place of the standard discs – and it weighed just over 9 tons, making it the heaviest double-deck motorbus yet seen on Britain's roads.

There were two Albion Lowlanders on show – an Alexander-bodied bus for BET subsidiary East Midland and a Northern Counties-bodied example for Central SMT. Alexander had overcome some of the problems of its first body which had been seen at the previous year's Scottish show, by raising the front upper deck windows. But Northern

The forward-entrance Routemaster which was exhibited at Earls Court in 1962 as London Transport RMF 1254 never actually entered revenue-earning service with LT. It was however demonstrated to a few provincial operators, including Halifax Corporation where it is seen in the spring of 1964 prior to a period on extended loan to British European Airways, as foreshadowed by its exterior advertisements.
Geoff Lumb

Counties showed how the job should be done, with a well-proportioned body which disguised the problems posed by the Lowlander's high driving position.

The other two half-cabs came from AEC. Routemaster production was continuing at Park Royal, the standard bus being a 27ft 6in-long 64-seater. London Transport had in 1961 taken delivery of two-dozen 30ft-long Routemasters, lengthened by the insertion of a short bay in the centre of the body. This increased the seating capacity to 72. At the 1962 Show, Park Royal exhibited a 30ft-long Routemaster which recognised the growing interest in forward-entrance buses outside London. This bus, London Transport RMF 1254, was exhibited as the ACV group announced that it was now in a position to sell Routemasters to operators outside the capital, this reflecting a drop in the rate of production for LT from an average of nine a week in 1960–61 to seven a week in 1962–63. BET was advised that a 72-seat Routemaster would cost around £6,700. RMF 1254 did not enter regular service in London, but it was demonstrated to three provincial operators – Liverpool, East Kent and Halifax – and then ran for a time with a luggage trailer on British European Airways' service from London to Heathrow Airport before being sold to Northern General in 1967.

Left The AEC Renown had the distinction of being the last new bus of traditional front-engined layout to be launched in Britain. It was a lowheight model and the successor to the Bridgemaster, and most were bought by BET companies, including East Yorkshire Motor Services. For EYMS the Park Royal body was modified with a slight inward slope to the upper deck pillars which allowed the bus to pass through the Beverley Bar. *Chris Aston*

Below AEC's Renown demonstrator visited operators throughout the country including some, like Edinburgh, where some time had elapsed since AEC had last supplied buses. Edinburgh remained with Leyland as its main supplier. The Renown was sold to Burwell & District in 1965. *Harry Hay*

coachbuilder. It used the same AV590 engine as had powered the Bridgemaster, but now with the option of AEC's two-pedal Monocontrol fluid transmission. Monocontrol Renowns had the gearbox mounted remotely under the stairs; only five were built. The Renown had leaf springs at the front, and rear air suspension. It used the same drop centre rear axle as the Bridgemaster, but with the differential on the offside rather than the nearside.

A manual-gearbox demonstrator with 71-seat forward-entrance Park Royal body in blue and cream livery was on display at Earls Court, supported by a similar bus with Monocontrol transmission in the demonstration park. This bus, 8071ML, had a 69-seat Park Royal body and carried the dark green livery of London Transport's country area, where it ran from Northfleet with fleet number RX1 for five months in 1963. AEC doubtless had an eye on LT's need to replace its lowbridge RLH-class Regent IIIs. The blue Renown demonstrator, 7552MX, was far-

travelled visiting a wide range of operators. The LT green demonstrator, incidentally, was the first Renown to be built and had a slightly higher bonnet line than those which came after it.

The Park Royal body for the Renown was not unlike that which had been fitted to the Bridgemaster – on 30ft-long buses the pillar spacing was the same – but it had just a bit more shape about it which eliminated some of the top-heavy slab-sided look of the older model.

Just as BET had been the strongest supporter of the Bridgemaster, so too it was with the Renown. By the end of 1963 there were 57 in service – of which 47 were running for BET companies. These were City of Oxford and South Wales (both former Bridgemaster buyers) and North Western, where they were the company's first-ever new AEC double-deckers, although it had a sizeable fleet of Reliance single-deckers. North Western had previously been buying Dennis Lolines and had built up a fleet of 50, making it the second

The final half-cab at the 1962 Show was a bus behind its time. AEC launched a new low-height model, the Renown, to replace the integral Bridgemaster which was built by Park Royal. In total just 180 Bridgemasters had been sold of which precisely two-thirds – 120 buses – went to BET subsidiaries City of Oxford, East Kent, East Yorkshire, South Wales and Western Welsh.

The Renown – reviving a name last used by AEC in the 1930s – was, according to the company's advertising of the time, a bus which "bristles with superior design features". It had a separate – and complex – chassis frame but could be bodied by any

Right The FLF-series became the most common Lodekka model from 1962, the year this bus joined the Cheltenham District fleet. It has the new style of radiator grille introduced that year. A non-standard blanking plate has been fitted on this vehicle which has the Cave-Browne-Cave heating system using radiators mounted on either side of the destination screen. A very small number of operators experimented with the Cave-Browne-Cave system, but the only manufacturers to use it on production vehicles were Bristol and Guy, on its Wulfrunian. *Chris Aston*

Below The first example of Alexander's lowheight bodywork for rear-engined chassis was built on the Scottish Bus Group's first Fleetline and delivered to Scottish Omnibuses towards the end of 1963. It had been ordered by Baxter's of Airdrie and was transferred to the Baxter fleet during 1964. During its brief period with Scottish Omnibuses it was used on one of the services linking Edinburgh and Glasgow. *Harry Hay*

AEC Renown deliveries

AEC demonstrators … … …	2
A1, Ardrossan … … … …	2
City of Oxford … … … …	43
East Yorkshire … … … …	34
King Alfred, Winchester … …	2
Leicester City Transport … …	13
Leigh Corporation … … …	18
North Western … … … …	33
Nottingham City Transport …	42
Red Rover, Aylesbury … …	1
Rotherham Corporation … …	3
Scottish Omnibuses … … …	1*
Smith, Barhead … … …	2
South Wales … … … …	19
West Bridgford … … … …	2
West Wales … … … …	1
Western Welsh … … … …	28
Wolverhampton Corporation …	5
Total … … … … …	**251**

* originally ordered as a Bridgemaster by Baxter, Airdrie.

largest user of the type after Aldershot & District. The North Western Renown order illustrated how some operators were still unsure about rear-engined buses since it was buying Renowns and Fleetlines at the same time. Five of the South Wales Renowns had Willowbrook bodies; all of the remaining Renowns for BET were bodied by Park Royal.

The other Renown buyers in 1963 were a mixed bunch. Leigh Corporation had four with rear-entrance East Lancs bodies, while three went to independents – two to Smith of Barrhead (which also had a pair of Bridgemasters) and one to West Wales, whose last new double-decker had been a Guy Wulfrunian. This was the last new double-deck bus for a Welsh independent fleet until the late 1990s. One Renown was delivered to Scottish Omnibuses. This followed the 1962 take-over by Scottish Omnibuses of the business of Baxter of Airdrie, which had had two Bridgemasters on order. One of the Bridgemasters was delivered to Scottish Omnibuses; the second went to Red Rover of Aylesbury and was replaced in the Scottish Omnibuses fleet by the Renown – in a vain attempt by AEC to coax the company away from Bristol Lodekkas.

The Bristol Lodekka was, perhaps surprisingly, the most numerous new double-decker in Britain in 1962 with 476 entering service putting it well ahead of the Routemaster (384) and the Atlantean (347). Overall, of course, Leyland was selling more double-deckers than any of its competitors – 772 (including Lowlanders) against AEC's 568.

The swing to rear-engined models was gaining momentum. In 1962 the Atlantean and Fleetline between them accounted for 20 per cent of new double-deck deliveries. In 1963 this figure rose to 30 per cent. The rise was solely down to the Fleetline, boosted by large orders from Belfast and Birmingham.

Glasgow took one Fleetline. In the second half of the 1950s Daimler had supplied 200 buses to Scotland's biggest municipal fleet and clearly hoped to retain a share of Glasgow's business. It didn't, and the Fleetline remained a one-off in the increasingly Leyland-dominated Glasgow fleet. Warrington tried rear-engined buses in 1963, taking nine Fleetlines with handsome East Lancs bodies, but reverted to rear-entrance exposed-radiator Leyland PD2s in 1964. Warrington's Fleetlines were the first to be bodied by East Lancs.

Rotherham Corporation nearly went rear-engined in 1963, with an order for three Fleetlines – but had a rethink and continued buying front-engined Daimlers instead. It would be 1967 before Rotherham bought Fleetlines.

The first new rear-engined bus for the Scottish Bus Group entered service in 1963. This was a Daimler Fleetline which had been ordered by Baxter of Airdrie. It had a lowheight Alexander body and was delivered to Scottish Omnibuses.

In the BET group Fleetlines were delivered to Maidstone & District, PMT, Trent and Tynemouth (all of which had previously taken Atlanteans), and to North Western, where they were being delivered at the same time as AEC Renowns. Perhaps of greater significance was the entry into service of 50 Fleetlines with Midland Red – its first rear-engined double-deckers, and the first 'deckers from an outside supplier since its batch of 100 Leyland Titans ten years earlier.

With the Fleetlines for BET came some new body suppliers – Northern Counties at Maidstone & District, and Alexander at PMT and Midland Red. The Midland Red Fleetlines had full-height bodies to the Glasgow style, but with flat glass windscreens on both decks. They marked Alexander's biggest order to date from an English company.

A problem in the early days of rear-engined bus operation was damage to the skirt panels in the wheelbase caused by high kerbs as drivers failed to take a wide enough sweep when turning left. The Alexander-bodied Fleetlines for Midland Red addressed this problem by having separate shallow skirt panels – with the join neatly masked by a polished moulding strip. It was an idea most operators and body-builders would develop to help keep accident repair costs down, although usually without going to the expense of covering the join with an elegant polished moulding.

Sales of new double-deckers to small inde-

pendents in the early 1960s were generally only just in double figures. A few bought Fleetlines – in 1963 Beckett of Bucknall (delivered just before the company was taken over by PMT) and Burwell & District. Burwell & District went to Willowbrook for its bodywork, making this the first rear-engined bus to be bodied by that builder.

At the start of 1963 Leyland announced a range of modifications to the Atlantean with the PDR1/1 MkII, although the MkII designation was not widely used. These included a three-piece engine cover in place of the original single-piece unit, revisions to the O.600 engine which brought a slight increase in power (up from 125 to 130bhp), the adoption of an SCG fluid-friction clutch in place of the original centrifugal clutch and changes to the engine mountings which allowed the gearbox to be replaced without removing the engine.

Gearbox failures were not uncommon on early Atlanteans. This was caused at first by inadequate sealing which allowed the two different oils used in the gearbox and the angle-drive to mix. The solution – to have a common system with the same oil in both units – didn't quite work either, as it led to oil being drawn out of the gearbox and pumped into the angle drive, again leading to gearbox failure.

However not all operators were geared up to deal with the maintenance requirements of rear-engined buses. A high incidence of gearbox failures on early Glasgow Corporation Atlanteans was in part down to the operator trying to save money by repairing and re-installing failed seals rather than replacing them.

The Atlantean was winning new business too. Bury took 15 in 1963, with Liverpool-style Metro-Cammell bodies. Leicester's first rear-engined buses were three Atlanteans in 1963 – although it would stay with front-engined models until 1968. Portsmouth went for the Atlantean in a big way, taking 35 in 1963 largely to replace the city's trolleybus system which closed that year.

Bolton switched from Titans in 1962 to Atlanteans in 1963 and did so with some style. General manager Ralph Bennett – who had been at Bolton since 1960 and whose name will crop up again – specified bodywork by East Lancs which was well-proportioned with deep windows on both decks and attractive side mouldings. These were MkII models which allowed Bennett to have fairings fitted above the engine, as pioneered by Northern Counties on its first Fleetline bodies. They also had translucent panels in the upper deck ceiling. The result was as far removed from previous generations of Bolton bus as can be

imagined. With the East Lancs-bodied Atlanteans came some with Liverpool-style Metro-Cammell bodies, but with external mouldings to suit Bolton's livery layout.

Independents buying their first Atlanteans were two local to Leyland – Bamber Bridge Motor Services and Fishwick and, on the other side of the Pennines, South Yorkshire Motors of Pontefract. All three operators specified lowbridge Weymann bodywork.

Scottish independent Graham's of Paisley backed both rear-engined models, taking one Fleetline and one Atlantean in 1963, both with Alexander bodies. By 1973 Graham's would have bought another 12 Fleetlines, but only one more Atlantean. The Gardner engine of the Fleetline provided continuity with the Guy Arabs which formed the bulk of Graham's fleet.

While the Lowlander was not the success Leyland might have hoped for, it did find its way into a few English fleets which had been running lowbridge buses. BET subsidiaries Ribble and East Midland switched to Lowlanders from Atlanteans with lowbridge bodies. Ribble's had Alexander bodies with full-width cabs, designed to emulate the fleet's PD3 Titans but not quite managing it thanks to a bulbous bonnet assembly.

Two municipal fleets took Lowlanders in 1963 – Luton and Southend. Luton had 16 and had been a Leyland buyer until it bought two Dennis Lolines in 1960. The Lowlander failed to impress Luton and its next double-deck order, in 1965, saw a switch back to Dennis. The Lowlander had a similar effect at Southend. Here it followed half-a-dozen

Above **Bolton Corporation was among the pioneers of a new look for rear-engined buses, taking not just the appearance of the body into consideration, but the livery application too. East Lancs built the bodies on most Bolton Atlanteans and these were well-proportioned with equal depth windows on both decks and peaked domes. These were early MkII PDR1/1s which had a lift-up centre section on the engine cover. This allowed the fitment of fairings to conceal the bustle-effect of the engine compartment. Nice touches include the shape of the wheelarches, body mouldings to suit the livery and the forward-angled frame for the first upper-deck side window, a typical early 1960s design theme. This is a 1965 bus.** Chris Aston

Below **When Ribble decided to buy Lowlanders rather than lowbridge Atlanteans in 1964 it presumably found that its most recent double-deck body supplier, Metro-Cammell, was unable or unwilling to body the new low-frame chassis. So it turned to Alexander, which was bodying large numbers of Lowlanders for SBG companies. To match the fully-fronted PD3s run by Ribble, Alexander fitted a full-width cab to the Lowlanders.** John Robinson

Bridgemasters in a predominantly Leyland fleet. After taking one batch of Lowlanders, Southend went back to PD3s – plus some high-capacity standee Leopards. At least Leyland's salesmen could console themselves that they had retained Southend's custom.

An order for 15 Lowlanders for Walsall Corporation had been announced by Leyland in 1962, but this was later described as having been postponed, which turned out to be a euphemism for cancelled. They would have had MCW group bodies.

In fact 1963 was, on the face of it, a good year for the Lowlander with over 200 entering service. This high figure was in part the result of late deliveries to Scottish Bus Group companies – and it actually represented 75 per cent of all Lowlander sales. The 1963 figure – 212 – compared with just 22 new Lowlanders entering service in 1964. Lowlanders were delivered to most Scottish Bus Group subsidiaries: the three Alexander companies created in 1961, Fife, Midland and Northern, plus Central SMT and Western SMT. Only Scottish Omnibuses (standardised on Lodekkas) and Highland Omnibuses (which wasn't buying new double-deckers) escaped. Northern's two Lowlanders in 1963 were its last new half-cabs; from 1964 the company's new buses would be single-deckers and its double-deck requirement would be met by older vehicles transferred from other SBG companies.

Double-deck deliveries in the period under review peaked at 2,723 in 1963, with Leyland models accounting for just over one third of deliveries in that year. From that point there started a steady decline – to a low of just 1,121 in 1968.

There were a number of reasons for both the peak and the decline. The peak had in part been fuelled by the normal replacement cycle for buses – averaging around 15 years. Work back 15 years from 1963 and you find yourself in the middle of the heavy postwar investment being made by bus operators trying to catch up with replacement programmes which had either slowed down or come to a halt during World War II. Postwar double-deck deliveries in the UK had peaked at almost 5,200 vehicles in 1950, a figure which includes nearly 300 trolleybuses.

The decline was brought about by a change of legislation – the relaxation of the length limits in July 1961 which allowed the operation of buses up to 36ft long (and, incidentally, increased the maximum width from 8ft to 8ft 2½in). This affected double-deck design, as bodybuilders such as Alexander used the relaxed limits to build bodies on Atlanteans which were just over 30ft long. But more significantly it focused operators' attention on the possibility of making greater use of single-deckers.

A 36ft-long single-deck bus could seat up to 53 and for some of the BET companies which were quick to order 36-footers that was the same capacity as the 15-year-old lowbridge buses they would replace. There was also strong interest in bus-operating practices in mainland Europe. One of the first visible signs of this was an exhibit at the 1961 Scottish Motor Show – a 36ft-long Leyland Leopard with three-door Alexander bodywork for Edinburgh Corporation. This had a wide entrance door in the rear overhang with space for a seated conductor, and two narrow exit doors – one in the centre, the other at the front. It seated 35 – reduced to 33 before the bus entered service – and had space for 30 standing passengers.

Having a seated conductor which all passengers had to pass meant that there should be no missed fares – a common problem on busy buses. To minimise loading time at stops there was a large standing area at the back where boarding passengers were herded together before filing past the conductor.

It was an interesting idea, but it was soon overtaken by a better one – having the driver collect the fares. One-man-operation (there

A few Crossley DD42s were bought new by independents. These included Lanarkshire operators Baxter of Airdrie and Duncan of Law. New to Duncan in 1947, this Crossley-bodied bus was later operated by Love of Lesmahagow in whose ownership it is seen in 1964. The postwar surge in bus buying led to double-deck deliveries hitting a peak in 1963 when buses such as this were being replaced in large numbers. Geoff Lumb

Not quite what it seems, this 1962-registered CVD6 in the AA fleet started life in 1950 as a Plaxton-bodied coach. It was rebodied by Northern Counties in 1962 and fitted with a unique new-look front incorporating the style of Daimler badge fitted to Fleetlines. Harry Hay

were very few women bus drivers at this time) was far from new, but it tended to be restricted to quiet routes. A few municipals ran one-man buses – often of dual-door layout – based on mid-engined chassis such as the AEC Reliance.

Leading the field was Reading Corporation, which had been running one-man Reliances with 60-passenger (34-seat) dual-door Burlingham bodies from 1957 and had two dozen in operation by 1962, making up almost a quarter of the fleet. Reading's use of one-man-operation was prompted by difficulties in recruiting staff. Portsmouth, too, explored one-man-operation with standee buses and by 1963 had 29 Leyland Tiger Cubs and Leopards with two-door Weymann bodywork in service. Here as in many other places there was trade

union resistance and while the first were delivered in October 1959 they didn't actually enter service until April 1960, after the best part of six months of negotiation on wage rates secured a 22 per cent one-man-operation allowance for their drivers. From 1962 all of Aberdare's new buses were one-man-operated single-deckers.

Sunderland Corporation, too, was exploring one-man-operation and in 1961–62 had added 14 two-door Reliances to its fleet, following these in 1963–64 with three Atkinsons with dual-door Marshall bodies. Atkinson, based in Walton-le-Dale, just outside Preston, had never been a big name in the UK bus business and these were its last deliveries to a British operator. They were PM746H chassis with mid-mounted Gardner engines.

Bodywork on high-frame mid-engined chassis had a three-step entrance, and it was a new breed of low-floor rear-engined models which was about to create increased interest in one-man-operation – at this time only permissible on single-deckers. Leyland's chief engineer, John McHugh, in a paper to a transport conference in 1961 put forward the idea of a light-weight rear-engined 36ft single-decker using an O.400 engine, air suspension, disc brakes and 15in wheels. His vision of PSV19XX, as he described it, included a backbone chassis, a plastic body with room for 48 seats and 27 standees, and an unbelievable low weight of 3 tons 5cwt. It may have been a kite flying exercise, but the 36ft standee single-decker was coming.

However first off the mark – albeit to a false start – was Daimler. At the 1962 Commercial Motor Show Daimler exhibited a

36ft-long chassis, the SRD6. The front section of the chassis was similar in concept to the Fleetline, but at the rear there was a horizontal 125bhp 8.6-litre Daimler CD6 engine. This was located transversely, and drove through Daimler's four-speed semi-automatic gearbox and an angle drive to a Fleetline drop-centre rear axle. There were also plans for a Gardner-engined version.

To ensure reasonable access to the auxiliaries the engine had to be turned round in the chassis, with the drive being taken from what would have been the front. This in turn meant modifying the engine so that it rotated in the opposite direction from normal. The radiator was located at the front – unlike the Fleetline which had its radiator alongside the engine. Leaf suspension was fitted. However the SRD6 was soon forgotten. Daimler diesel engine production was at an all-time low and would soon end. By the 1964 Show, Daimler would be back with an all-new single-deck chassis.

Next in line was Bristol, with the RE. A prototype RELL6G with 54-seat ECW bus body entered service with United Auto at the end of 1962 – the first modern rear-engined single-decker in Britain. The chassis type code indicated Rear Engine, Long wheelbase, Low chassis frame. The RE had a choice of Gardner 6HLW or 6HLX engines, mounted horizontally at the rear. To accommodate the length of the 6HLX, Bristol adopted an ingenious layout which involved two propeller shafts. One took the drive from the engine to the gearbox, which was located ahead of the drop-centre rear axle, while the second brought the drive back again from gearbox to axle. As with Daimler, production of in-house engines was on the wane at Bristol and there was no Bristol engine option on the RE.

The RE had air suspension as standard – its first truly successful application to a British bus chassis. Series production, initially of RELH high-framed coach chassis, started in the autumn of 1963 and it would in fact be late summer 1964 before more RELL buses would take to the road. By the end of that year there

were 40 production RELLs in operation with United Auto, West Yorkshire, Thames Valley and Lincolnshire – all 54-seaters bodied by ECW.

Blackburn-based coachbuilder East Lancs was taken over by the John Brown Engineering group in 1963 which set up a subsidiary in Sheffield, Neepsend Coachworks, to provide extra capacity. Neepsend built bodies on both front- and rear-engined chassis which were indistinguishable from those produced at Blackburn, initially using kits supplied by

East Lancs but later building from East Lancs' drawings. There is a tale – apocryphal, perhaps – that the East Lancs management harboured suspicions that John Brown planned to close the Blackburn factory and transfer all production to Sheffield, and that to protect their position they ensured that the drawings which they supplied were never 100 per cent accurate. Be that as it may, the Neepsend factory – which took its name from the part of Sheffield in which it was located – closed in 1967.

KING OF THE ROAD

IN 1962 a merger had taken place which proved to be pivotal in the development of British bus manufacturing. The partners were Leyland and Associated Commercial Vehicles, the holding company for AEC, Park Royal and Roe. Leyland was the dominant partner, and in 1963 a new umbrella organisation was announced – the Leyland Motor Corporation.

It came at a time when urban operators were showing growing interest in one-man-operated standee single-deckers as an alternative to double-deckers. This would depress demand for double-deckers as the 1960s progressed.

One of the first fruits of the merger was the use of the same chassis frame for two new rear-engined single-deckers – the Leyland Panther and AEC Swift.

The Panther was first, being announced in February 1964, and it featured the horizontal Leyland O.600 engine as fitted to the Leopard. For bus use the Panther had Leyland's four-speed Pneumocyclic gearbox. The Swift followed at the 1964 Commercial Motor Show in September and used AEC's new AH505 engine, developed from the previous AH470 but with its displacement raised from 7.68 to 8.2 litres. The Panther had a front-mounted radiator; the Swift had its radiator at the rear.

The positioning of the radiator remote from the engine was a departure from normal Leyland practice and it quickly became apparent that there was a less than full understanding of the implications of long water flows on engine cooling performance. Overheating was a problem, exacerbated on early models by the lack of a header tank to help maintain water levels.

Another problem was track rod failure. To achieve tight turning circles required a new approach to track rod design and this resulted in excessive pressure on the nearside track rod end. Unlikely as it may sound, the dynamics of the Panther were such that even with steering operating only on the offside wheel most defective buses made it back to base, often without the driver realising that he had a problem. This design defect would also affect long-wheelbase PDR2/1 Atlanteans.

At the 1964 Earls Court show there were six rear-engined single-deckers. AEC showed a Swift chassis (price £3,165) while Leyland had two Panthers on display. One had 42-seat dual-door bodywork by Alexander and was for Glasgow Corporation; the other was a Roe-bodied 45-seater for Hull, also with two doors. There was also a short Panther variant – the 33ft-long Panther Cub which had Leyland's O.400 engine and was for Manchester Corporation. It had a two-door Park Royal body, with 43 seats. The use of the smaller O.400 engine was essential to meet legislation on the length of the rear overhang, but within Leyland there was a feeling that it was insufficiently powerful. However Manchester was reported to have threatened to place an order with Daimler – its other key supplier – if Leyland did not produce a suitable model.

The Glasgow Panther had its Pneumocyclic gearbox replaced with a three-speed Voith automatic before entering service. Voith had a link up with Glasgow-based North British Locomotive Works, and was trying to promote its DIWAbus gearboxes in the UK. One was also fitted experimentally to a Western SMT PD3A Titan.

The bodies for the rear-engined single-deckers were all new. Alexander's, coded the W-type, used the front and rear windscreens of the Y-type coach, but all else was new. The generally similar Roe and Park Royal bodies for Hull and Manchester featured the attractive double-curvature windscreen developed by the BET group and fitted to virtually all of its single-deck buses and dual-purpose vehicles from 1963. The BET screen, as it became known, would be used by a wide range of builders over the next three decades.

And Daimler was back. It had abandoned the SRD6 and in its place revealed the Roadliner SRC6. Where AEC, Bristol and Leyland used horizontal versions of proven in-line six-cylinder engines, Daimler opted for a compact V6 unit from an American manufacturer hitherto unknown in the British bus industry: Cummins. This engine was just 33.5in long and therefore occupied little space within the body. The drive was taken to an Eaton rear axle by way of a four-speed Daimatic gearbox.

Daimler launched its new chassis claiming somewhat half-heartedly that it was "almost avant-garde in its design approach and excecution" and pointing to the company having "amassed a truly formidable amount of expertise and operating experience over several million miles and covering every aspect of rear-engined chassis design and operation" with the Fleetline.

The Roadliner had air suspension as standard (with Metalastik rubber or conventional springs as an option) and originally had a front-mounted radiator, although this was soon resited at the rear. It was designed for 36ft-long bodywork and while a 33ft model was publicised, none were built.

On show at Earls Court were a Roadliner chassis, and a 50-seat Marshall-bodied bus for PMT. (There was also a Duple-bodied coach, demonstrating the Roadliner's flexibility.) The Cummins engine was in effect fitted under the rear seat of the Roadliner bus, which had a ramped, step-free floor. Most early rear-engined single-deckers had an almost flat floor at the front, with a step up over the rear axle – a layout which saw many bodybuilders adopt a stepped waistline with deeper windows in the front section of the body than at the rear.

While low-frame rear-engined single-deckers grabbed most attention, there were conventional mid-engined models too, including a Leopard for West Hartlepool

Swift
U.K.

Corporation with two-door Strachans body, designed for one-man-operation. The West Hartlepool fleet at this time was made up of half-cab double-deckers – but only two more would be bought, in 1965, as West Hartlepool turned to one-man single-deckers in a big way.

The interest in one-man operation by urban operators was largely created by the need to introduce operating economies in the face of a steady decline in bus use. In some areas it also helped alleviate the effects of staff shortages at a time of relatively high employment.

The Manchester Panther Cub was one of 20, and the model had been developed by Leyland to meet Manchester's concerns about operating a 36ft-long single-decker in busy city streets – a concern that one other major urban operator, London Transport, would have done well to have taken note of. In the event the Panther Cub proved to be more trouble than it was worth, rather as Leyland had feared. Only 97 were built, and Manchester's were withdrawn after just seven years in service.

The move to the new generation of rear-engined single-deckers started slowly. While there were economic pressures in their favour, there were counter-pressures too. The introduction of one-man operation was generally opposed by trade unions, anxious to preserve jobs. Most operators were restricted to a maximum of 45 seats on one-man buses, as set in a national agreement with the Transport and General Workers Union. This saw companies such as Ribble having just 45 seats in some 36ft-long Leopards which would otherwise have been 53-seaters, while Maidstone & District actually removed eight seats from some of its 53-seat Leopards so that they could be run as one-man buses.

There was passenger reaction too. Although most urban journeys were relatively short, bus users generally equated payment of

a fare with the provision of a seat. Crush loading was accepted by rail-based commuters in London, but not by bus passengers in the provinces. And to cut delays on pay-as-you-enter buses, some operators opted for simplified farescales – for which read higher fares for most users.

Against this background double-deck sales remained healthy with deliveries of Fleetlines overtaking those of the Atlantean for the first time – 412 against 293 – although the Atlantean would regain the lead in 1965 and 1966. This performance made the Fleetline Britain's best-selling bus in 1964. In all 526 Daimler double-deckers took to Britain's streets that year, putting Daimler just behind Leyland with 578 deliveries (including 22 Lowlanders). This was a remarkable performance for Daimler, who as recently as 1960 had been something of an also-ran behind AEC, Leyland and Bristol with sales volumes which placed it in the second division alongside Dennis and Guy.

Among the Fleetlines were more short examples for Walsall. These were slightly longer than the 1962 Show bus at 27ft 6in, with a short front overhang and the driver now located just ahead of the front axle. The seating capacity had been increased from 64 to

70. This made much more sense and was a remarkable figure for a compact bus achieved in part by having a two-seat inward-facing bench over the front nearside wheel. A forward-ascending staircase was located directly opposite the sliding entrance door. Most of the exterior panelling was made of colour-impregnated Filon. This was a glass fibre material which had also been tried by Midland Red on one of its D9 double-deckers. It was lighter than metal and, in theory at least, eliminated the need for repainting.

Leyland was understandably concerned about losing business to the Fleetline, and came up with a lowheight Atlantean, the PDR1/2, by using the Lowlander's drop-centre rear axle driving through the Daimler gearbox fitted to the Fleetline. The PDR1/2 could not be fitted with the optional 153bhp O.680 engine which had been used in small numbers of PDR1/1s – the revised drive train could not handle the higher power and torque. Indeed even with the O.600 the PDR1/2 proved a troublesome vehicle with rear axle and gearbox failures leading to major rectification campaigns.

The first PDR1/2s entered service towards the end of 1964 and the model was initially bought by operators who saw benefits in elim-

were buying Atlanteans and Fleetlines – so it is in some ways ironic that the move towards the widespread use of one-man-operated rear-engined single-deckers in place of crew-operated double-deckers gathered momentum in the capital.

The first of a new breed of one-man buses for operation in London appeared in 1966 with the arrival of 15 AEC Merlins. The Merlin was a heavy-duty version of the Swift, powered by AEC's 11.3-litre AH691 engine in place of the 8.2-litre AH505. In April 1966 London Transport introduced six Merlins to a new limited-stop Red Arrow service between Marble Arch and Victoria Station. Their two-door Strachans bodies had just 25 seats (in the raised rear section) with space for 48 standing passengers. The service had a flat fare of 6d with payment being made by dropping a coin into a slot alongside one of two turnstiles located immediately to the rear of the driver.

The other nine Merlins were 45-seaters intended for country area services. Eight of these were rebuilt as 25-seaters, and instead entered service as Red Arrows in 1967. The last remained as a country bus, finally entering service in the autumn of 1968.

This was the start of LT's brief attachment to standee buses, and its famous Bus Reshaping Plan of 1966 envisaged the widespread use of such vehicles throughout London. The plan had been developed to combat two major problems facing LT – continuing staff shortages and worsening traffic congestion.

By adopting one-man-operation wherever possible, LT hoped to overcome its manpower shortage. And by breaking long routes into shorter sections it hoped to counter the worst effects of traffic congestion. Short routes would have a flat fare and automatic fare collection equipment, while on longer routes graduated fares would be retained but there was the hope that electronic fare collection equipment could be developed which would allow passengers to buy stored-value tickets for use on both buses and the Underground. This was an idea ahead of its time and, as LT would find out, ahead of the available technology too.

Initial orders were placed for 650 Merlins as the first step in providing Londoners with a modern transport system, based on short suburban route networks converging on Underground stations. The reality would fall somewhat short of LT's high ideals. In the meantime Routemaster deliveries continued apace, with 72-seat 30ft-long versions taking over from the original 64-seat model from the start of 1966.

In 1965 almost 40 per cent of all new double-deckers entering service in Britain were rear-engined. Take out London's Routemasters and the substantial numbers of Lodekkas being delivered to the Tilling and

Nottingham bought AEC Renowns and Leyland Atlantean PDR 1/2s to take advantage of their low-floor capability, rather than because they could be built to a low overall height. After buying Fleetlines in 1962 and 1963, Nottingham bought its first Atlanteans in 1964. By 1967 it would have 99 PDR 1/2s in service. This 1965 bus has a 77-seat Northern Counties body with distinctive Nottingham features including the BET-style windscreen and a forward-inclined destination display. Royston Morgan

inating the step towards the rear of the lower saloon rather than by those who needed lowheight bodywork. The first users were Sheffield and Nottingham, quickly joined by Manchester – which took 72 in 1965 – and by Coventry, a new customer for Leyland. The Nottingham vehicles included the first Atlanteans to have bodywork by Northern Counties.

The Coventry order caused some controversy. Coventry Corporation's fleet was made up almost entirely of locally-built Daimlers, but its first order for rear-engined buses called for 22 Fleetlines and 22 Atlanteans. The Atlantean order was not repeated. Presumably satisfied that it had shown Daimler that its business couldn't be taken for granted, Coventry then standardised on the Fleetline.

Coventry's body supplier, Metro-Cammell, fared less well. It had supplied all of Coventry's double-deck bodywork since 1948, but after the last Orion bodies on a batch of CVG6s in 1963 it would supply no more. The 44 rear-engined buses delivered in 1965 had

Willowbrook bodies – that builder's biggest single 1960s double-deck order – and subsequent deliveries would see a variety of other bodybuilders' products arriving in Coventry. With the switch to rear engines came a brighter new livery with more cream and less maroon.

In the East Midlands, Nottingham had been buying rear-engined double-deckers since 1962 and by the end of 1965 had over 130 in service – which makes the delivery of its last half-cabs in that year seem all the more unusual. These were 42 AEC Renowns with full-height forward-entrance bodywork by Weymann. The fitment of full-height bodywork on a low-frame chassis allowed the provision of a single-step entrance – thinking which was 30 years ahead of its time – and generous interior headroom.

Nottingham was also developing its own distinctive style of bodywork, premiered at the 1964 Earls Court Show by a Northern Counties-bodied Atlantean which had a BET-style windscreen with the destination display fitted to a forward-sloping panel immediately above it.

By 1964 all but one of the big municipal fleets were running at least some rear-engined buses, even if a few remained to be convinced that it was the best way forward. The exception was Leeds, and in 1964 it went with the flow, putting ten Fleetlines into service – although it would continue to buy AEC Regents until 1966.

London was still taking delivery of Routemasters – while most other major cities

Scottish groups, and rear-engined buses were actually out-selling front-engined models in those fleets where operators had real choice in the buses they bought.

Even London Transport could not ignore the gathering pace of change, and in 1965 it took delivery of 58 rear-engined double-deckers: 50 Atlanteans and eight Fleetlines. All had 72-seat Park Royal bodies of rather conservative appearance, ignoring the trend away from boxy BET-inspired bodywork in places as diverse as Bolton, Glasgow, Liverpool and Sunderland.

The Atlanteans were red central area buses; the Fleetlines were green for country area operation – although both types were tried in both areas. One Fleetline was fitted with a Cummins V6 engine in 1967, which involved extending the engine compartment to accommodate the extra width of the vee-configuration engine. On central area services LT reported fuel consumption figures of 6.6mpg for its Atlanteans and 7.8mpg for the Fleetlines – the latter figure was the same as its 30ft-long RML-class Routemasters.

These standard buses were followed in 1966 by an intriguing might-have-been: a rear-engined Routemaster. This used a high degree of standard Routemaster body parts, but with a transverse 11.3-litre AEC AV691 engine. The body originally had fixed windows and a thermostatically-controlled heating and ventilation system. But following fire damage in 1967 this was replaced by conventional heaters and the body was fitted with wind-down quarter-drop windows as used on standard Routemasters. The rear-engined Routemaster initially operated alongside Atlanteans in central London.

That it never reached series production is not surprising. The Routemaster was a sophisticated and relatively expensive bus. No real effort had been made to sell front-engined Routemasters and the only deliveries outside LT were to BET subsidiary Northern General and to British European Airways, whose fleet was operated on BEA's behalf by LT.

By the time the rear-engined Routemaster appeared in 1966, the Atlantean had been in production for eight years and there were around 2,500 in service. The Fleetline had been in production for six years and was getting near to achieving 2,000 sales. Outside London, sales of AEC double-deckers were steadily dwindling – in part because there was no rear-engined model to compete with the Atlantean. Add to all this the formation of the Leyland Motor Corporation and Leyland's dominance in it, and it's easy to see that there would be little enthusiasm within LMC to produce an expensive model with limited sales potential to compete with the increasingly successful Atlantean in a market which looked as though it was about to forsake the double-decker anyway.

Above Strachans built this flamboyant body on an AEC Regent III for Delaine of Bourne in 1953. Similar mouldings had been used on a fully-fronted body the company had delivered to Highland Transport in 1951. Delaine operated in the finest independent tradition and its Regent looked as good when photographed in 1965 as it had when new. While it may have looked old-fashioned when compared with new Atlanteans and Fleetlines, it exuded an unmistakable touch of class. The chassis was a 9613S with synchromesh gearbox. Delaine would continue to buy distinctive double-deckers, including in the late 1950s the only examples to be built by Yeates of Loughborough who were supplying the company's single-deck bodywork at that time. *Geoff Lumb*

Below While a number of major fleet operators had broken away from the boxy appearance of early Atlanteans, when London Transport ordered its first rear-engined buses it specified plain-looking Park Royal bodies. These had a bit more shape than the very earliest bodies on Atlanteans, but compared unfavourably with buses being built for Glasgow and Liverpool, for example. There were 50 Atlanteans for London and they seated 72, the same as RML-class Routemasters. *Iain MacGregor*

Sales of AEC double-deckers were falling in the mid-1960s as operators switched to rear-engined models from Daimler and Leyland. This AEC Regent V joined the fleet of Garelochhead Coach Services in 1964 and had bodywork by Northern Counties. Full-fronted buses were never common in Scotland and this was the last to be bought new. For subsequent Regents Garelochhead reverted to the conventional half-cab layout. Harry Hay

And the final nail in the rear-engined Routemaster's coffin, were one needed, was LT's Bus Reshaping Plan which saw a reduced role for double-deckers in the future. Park Royal and AEC had planned to build three prototype rear-engined Routemasters – but only London's was actually completed.

The Routemasters for Northern General, 50 delivered in two batches in 1964–65, were 30ft-long forward-entrance buses, similar to the 1962 Commercial Motor Show exhibit – which migrated north to join the Northern General fleet at the start of 1967. They had Leyland O.600 engines – to provide some measure of standardisation with the company's Atlanteans – and were the first half-cabs for the Northern General group of companies since a batch of Leyland Titans in 1958. They were also the Northern General group's last half-cabs, and were in fact accompanied by Atlanteans which would continue to come until 1968 after which there was a switch to Fleetlines (and to single-deckers).

While some BET companies had been leaders in the move to rear-engined double-deckers, it did actually take 10 years for all companies in the group to make the change from front-engined to rear-engined 'deckers, which was in part a reflection of their relatively poor reliability when compared with conventional types. One company which didn't move to rear-engined 'deckers was Aldershot & District. In 1964–65 it added 50 Dennis Loline IIIs to its fleet – bringing to 141 the number of Lolines it operated (out of a total production run of 280) – and these were the company's last double-deckers.

Maidstone & District, which had been buying Atlanteans and Fleetlines, became one of the first BET companies to try rear-engined single-deckers in quantity with the delivery of 15 Panthers in 1965. These had Willowbrook bodies – twelve were 53-seaters but the last three had just 45 seats so that they could be used as one-man buses without breaking the national agreement in place with the TGWU. A further 50, again a mix of 45- and 53-seaters, followed in 1967.

Where the move to single-deckers did have a lasting effect was among some of the smaller municipal fleets which either bought their last double-deckers ever, or moved away from 'deckers for a very long time. As early as 1961 Barrow-in-Furness took delivery of its last double-deckers for 20 years with ten Massey-bodied PD2As. Morecambe's last, in 1962, were two similar buses. In 1964 Darlington took delivery of six Daimler CCG6s with open-platform Roe bodies, and then switched to Daimler single-deckers.

Exeter, which had standardised on Massey-bodied Titans – buying them at the rate of five a year – took its last in 1965. Also receiving their last double-deckers in 1965 were Lancaster (three PD2s), Luton (six Lolines) and West Bridgford (two Renowns, unusual in having semi-automatic gearboxes). West Monmouthshire Omnibus Board and Widnes Corporation would take their last 'deckers, PD2 Titans, in 1966.

By this time most bus operators had standardised on bodies which were 8ft – or in a few cases 2.5m – wide. But there were still very small numbers of 7ft 6in-wide double-deckers entering service. The last were Leyland Titans – three with Massey bodies and St Helens-style fronts for Colchester Corporation in 1964, followed by 12 with forward-entrance East Lancs bodies and exposed radiators for Warrington in 1965. Warrington's were its last Titans; Colchester took one more batch of PD2s, but 8ft wide, in 1966.

While conservatism played a part in some operators' decisions to stick with front-engined buses, there was a price penalty in

Among BET fleets, Maidstone & District was the biggest user of the Leyland Panther, building up a fleet of 95. Of these, 65 were bodied by Willowbrook and while all were suitable for use as 53-seaters, some were specified with just 45 seats to meet a trade union agreement which restricted the number of seats permissible in a one-man-operated bus. David Brown

buying rear-engined types – apart from any on-going increase in running costs. At the end of 1965 Leyland's price list showed that a PDR1/1 Atlantean cost £3,818, while a Titan PD3A/2 was listed at £3,667 – a difference of 4 per cent. A PSUR1/1 Panther cost £3,576. Leyland's cheapest double-deck chassis at this time was the PD2/37 (exposed radiator, synchromesh gearbox) costing £3,294. Specify a Pneumocyclic gearbox on a Titan and it cost an extra £237, while a new-look front added £47.

The 1965 Scottish Motor Show produced one surprise. The fitment of longer side windows on single-deck buses – or more commonly dual-purpose vehicles – had been becoming increasingly common since the start of the 1960s. At the Scottish show the concept of a big-windowed double-decker was unveiled. The bus was Edinburgh Corporation's first Atlantean, and it had a Glasgow-style Alexander body on which every second pillar was interrupted at waist-rail level on both decks to create extra-long windows. The effect was dramatic, and had been developed by Alexander in conjunction with Edinburgh general manager Ronald Cox. It also had engine shrouds, for the first time on an Alexander body.

It was one of 25 on order – an order which had been placed after comparative trials in service of three demonstrators – Daimler Fleetline 565CRW, Atlantean KTD551C and – surely a lost cause – Renown 7552MX. Interestingly, fuel consumption for the three demonstrators wasn't that different. The Renown was best at 8.56mpg, followed by the Fleetline at 8.25 and the Atlantean at 8.2. By comparison, a standard Edinburgh PD3 running alongside the demonstrators returned 8.46mpg.

The other bus exhibits at Kelvin Hall in 1965 were a second Glasgow Panther (the first had been at the 1964 Earls Court show) and a demonstration Daimler Roadliner with 50-seat BET-style Marshall body in what was claimed to be Western SMT colours – it was red and cream, but that was the limit of its resemblance to Western's livery. At this stage the Roadliner had yet to gather any significant in-service experience, although the idea of a V6 engine from a manufacturer unknown in Britain might have made operators a trifle wary.

In any event, it was down to Britain's biggest municipal operator, Birmingham, to take an alternative view of low-floor single-deck operation and it came up with a novel idea. It was committed to Fleetlines for its double-deck fleet: so why not use the Fleetline as a single-decker too?

And so in 1965 it took delivery of 24 CRG6 chassis which had 37-seat Marshall bodies. The chassis had a slightly longer wheelbase than normal, to give an overall length of 30ft

6in. With their low build and protruding engines they looked like cut-down double-deckers. The idea of using virtually the same chassis for both single- and double-deck buses was far from new. It had been standard practice since the late 1920s and had only come to an end at the start of the 1950s with the advent of new underfloor-engined single-deck designs.

The Scottish Bus Group had been slow to be convinced of the merits of rear-engined double-deckers. Its first new example, a Fleetline for Scottish Omnibuses in 1963, was an order inherited with the business of Baxter of Airdrie. However in 1965 an order was placed for 54 for Western SMT, all with lowheight Alexander bodies. A further 38 would follow in 1966. Other SBG companies buying double-deckers in these years continued to take Lodekkas or Lowlanders.

Above **Edinburgh Corporation pioneered the use of panoramic windows on double-deckers, adopting them as standard on its Alexander-bodied Atlanteans from 1967. The result was striking – even if the upper and lower deck windows did appear to be out of step on the offside. The only ventilation on this 1969 bus was provided by lift-up hatches on the roof. It is one-man-operated.**
Iain MacGregor

Below **The Scottish Bus Group's first big order for Fleetlines was for Western SMT in 1965, and the Fleetline with Alexander body soon became a common sight not just with Western, but also with Alexander (Fife) and Alexander (Midland). The lowheight version of the Alexander body had equal-depth windows on both decks and was among the most attractive designs of its time.**
Iain MacGregor

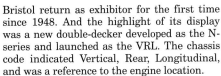

BY 1966 the front-engined double-decker was in terminal decline – except in the Tilling group, where the two remaining Lodekka models, the FS and FLF, continued to be supplied in quantity – over 330 in that year, although this number would drop to under 250 in 1967. However there were signs of fresh thinking at Bristol and, coincidentally, a change in ownership which would also affect not just Bristol, but ECW too.

The change came about as the result of a share exchange with Leyland in 1965, which saw Leyland take a 25 per cent stake in the two state-owned manufacturers. This would later be increased to 50 per cent, in 1969. The Transport Holding Company in turn took a 30 per cent share in Park Royal. The logic behind Leyland's minority stakeholding – which was encouraged by the Labour government which included Bristol MP Tony Benn – was the release of both Bristol and ECW from the restrictions set out in the 1947 Transport Act which only allowed them to supply state-owned operators. For over 15 years the vast majority of ECW's output had been on Bristol chassis and, conversely all Bristols, apart from a small number of coaches for Western SMT

(and, later, for Scottish Omnibuses), had been bodied by ECW.

It also meant that, in theory, any operator could buy Bristol Lodekkas, which immediately weakened the position of the Dennis Loline. At the start of 1966 Bristol announced a new Lodekka chassis, coded LDL, which had a deeper chassis frame with conventional channel-section side members and had the wheelbase reduced to 18ft 6in (from the standard 19ft 2½in on an FLF) so that it would be easier for bodybuilders to adapt their existing designs to fit. A bodied LDL would have been about 14ft 1in high and Bristol was offering the choice of 135bhp Gardner 6LX, 112bhp Gardner 6LW or 125bhp Leyland O.600 engines. However by this time sales of front-engined buses were quite clearly on the wane. No LDL Lodekka chassis were built and no ECW-bodied Lodekkas were sold to companies outside the Tilling and Scottish groups, although Lowestoft Corporation placed a provisional order for two FS models which was not turned in to a firm order. The Loline continued to find a small number of buyers.

The 1966 Commercial Motor Show saw

Bristol return as exhibitor for the first time since 1948. And the highlight of its display was a new double-decker developed as the N-series and launched as the VRL. The chassis code indicated Vertical, Rear, Longitudinal, and was a reference to the engine location.

Unlike the Atlantean and Fleetline with their transverse engines, Bristol had chosen to install its engine at the offside rear of the chassis. This eliminated the angle drive necessary with transverse engines, with the drive being taken straight from the Gardner 6LX engine via a semi-automatic SCG gearbox to a drop-centre rear axle with the differential located to the offside. It also meant a relatively long rear overhang. Planned engine options were the 150bhp Gardner 6LX or the new 180bhp 6LXB, and the Leyland O.600 and O.680.

The chassis had a conventional full-length ladder-type frame but from a point just ahead of the rear wheels a substantial perimeter frame swept up over the wheels and then dropped down behind them to accommodate the engine. To provide some balance for the offset engine, the VRL's batteries were located immediately behind the front nearside wheel, under a longitudinal seat. The radiator was at the front, as on the RE single-decker.

Where the Atlantean and Fleetline had hinged covers to give access to the engine, the 80-seat (45 up, 35 down) ECW body fitted to the VRL had removable access panels on the side and rear. The body was based on that fitted to the FLF, but was just over 33ft long – one of the first 'deckers of this length – with a

Bristol's first rear-engined double-decker was the VRL and two prototypes with ECW bodywork entered service in 1967. These were the first rear-engined 'deckers to be bodied by ECW and the body bore a strong resemblance to that fitted to contemporary FLFs. It also showed that it wasn't necessary to adopt curved glass windscreens to achieve a neat and attractive frontal appearance. The blank panel at the offside rear is above the engine compartment. Central SMT ran this bus until 1970 when it joined the Bristol Omnibus fleet. It is seen passing the company's headquarters in Motherwell soon after entering service.
Iain MacGregor

neatly styled front end which had slight vertical curvature and flat glass windscreens. Having the longitudinal engine inside the body did away with the visual problem of the protruding rear engine. Inside the lower saloon the engine was enclosed in a box which occupied the space behind the offside rear wheels. On the nearside opposite the engine were two pairs of forward-facing double seats. There was an emergency exit on the rear of the bus behind the last pair of seats.

There were two VRLs at the 1966 Earls Court show. On the Bristol stand was a bus in the colours of Bristol Omnibus, while ECW showed a similar vehicle in the livery of Central SMT. The Central bus entered service in January 1967, followed in February by the Bristol Omnibus vehicle, running initially for Mansfield District. Both vehicles were in fact owned by Bristol Commercial Vehicles until 1970 when they were bought by Bristol Omnibus.

Bristol claimed that one of the advantages of the VRL was the ability to locate an exit doorway anywhere on the body – and, indeed, 25 were built for service in South Africa with a second doorway in the rear overhang. The chassis was available with an 18ft 6in wheelbase (instead of 16ft 2in) for bodywork up to 36ft long, and in this form would be bought for motorway coach services by Standerwick, the BET company which operated from the north-west of England to London. It could also in theory be bodied as a single-decker, but none were – although suitable designs existed on ECW's drawing boards.

For single-deck operation Bristol continued to supply the RE and there were two with ECW bodies at the 1966 Earls Court show. Both were for Tilling group companies – United Auto and, in the demonstration park, West Yorkshire. The latter had a two-door body.

The other exhibits at the 1966 show highlighted the varied approaches being adopted to urban bus design. The front-engined double-decker was not yet dead, although 1966 was the last year in which deliveries of new front-engined 'deckers would outnumber those of rear-engined layout – with a 55:45 split in favour of the traditional layout. In 1967 the balance was tipped – just – in favour of rear-engined models at 51:49.

So 1966 was the last show to see a Leyland Titan and an AEC Regent. The Regent was for South Wales Transport and had a half-cab 64-seat Willowbrook body. It was the first of a batch of 18, which would be SWT's last new double-deckers until the mid-1970s. SWT had bought 216 Regent Vs since 1955, making it the biggest user of the type within the BET group. The bus was on Willowbrook's stand, and was the last half-cab to appear at an Earls Court show.

The Titan was a Southdown PD3 with Northern Counties body which differed from previous deliveries in having a BET-style curved windscreen. This feature echoed Northern Counties' pioneering styling work with curved windscreens on Regent Vs and a Loline for Barton Transport in 1960, and had previously been tried on one of Southdown's 1965 delivery of PD3s. To fit the bigger windscreen the radiator had to be resited under the staircase. The 1966 show vehicle not only had a BET screen, but had panoramic windows too.

Southdown would take its last PD3s in 1967 – with panoramic windows but conventionally-located radiators – and these would be the last Titans for the BET group. They were also the only front-engined buses to be fitted with bodywork incorporating panoramic windows. In fact 1967 marked the end of the delivery of front-engined double-deckers to BET with City of Oxford, East Kent, South

Above **Guy Arabs were popular with some of the small operators in the Doncaster area, including Store (Reliance) of Stainforth which took delivery of this Arab V in 1966. Like most buses bought by Doncaster's independents, it had a Roe body.**
Stewart J Brown

Free to supply companies outside the state-owned sector, Bristol quickly put an RE demonstrator on the road. A Leyland-engined RELL6L, it had a two-door ECW body with just 35 seats but room for 40 standees. It demonstrated to Glasgow Corporation in 1967. Iain MacGregor

Wales and Southdown being the recipients of, between them, 25 Titans, 20 Regent Vs and four Renowns. Production of BMMO's distinctive D9 had ceased in 1966.

Following Edinburgh's lead at the 1965 Scottish show, Leeds had a Roe body with panoramic windows at Earls Court in 1966, developed by Roe in conjunction with Leeds general manager Thomas Lord. It also used Alexander's curved front windscreens on both decks. It was built on the new long-wheelbase Fleetline CRG6LX/33 chassis but despite its extra length seated just 78 and can thus be seen as one of the first vehicles in which high carrying capacity was matched to some attempt to improve passenger comfort. While Daimler showed one of Britain's first completed 33ft-long double-deckers, Leyland displayed a 33ft Atlantean chassis, coded PDR2/1. It had an 18ft 6in wheelbase and was mechanically similar to the PDR1/1 but was only available with the O.680 engine and not the less-powerful O.600. It would be 1968 before any PDR2/1s entered service.

While body styles were becoming ever more standardised, there were still some relatively small fleets having buses bodied to their own designs. One such was Oldham Corporation, and a Roe-bodied Atlantean at the show illustrated Oldham's unusual styling with a prominent peak which gave it something of a top-heavy look. This was one of the fleet's first Atlanteans and it followed ten Roe-bodied PD3s in 1963 which had been Oldham's first 30ft-long double-deckers and were the only ones in the fleet of forward-entrance layout.

Another style of Roe bodywork could be seen at Earls Court on a low-height PDR1/2 Atlantean for West Riding. West Riding had persevered with the Guy Wulfrunian and had taken a final batch of 30 in 1965. For 1966 it cancelled an order for a further 25

Wulfrunians and instead had 25 Atlanteans. These had 76-seat Roe bodies with Alexander-style curved windscreens on both decks. With the Atlanteans West Riding also bought 10 single-deck buses – Daimler Roadliners with Plaxton bodies.

It's hard not to feel sympathy with West Riding's engineers. There they were coping with a fleet of Wulfrunians and what do they get next? Roadliners. It's a sign of the trouble they caused that when they were due for recertification after seven years in service all the Roadliners were sold. The majority of the Wulfrunians met a similar fate with few running for more than seven years at West Riding and many not even lasting that length of time. Those that were still in service in 1969 had eight seats removed from the front of the upper deck to reduce loading on the front suspension which was wearing tyres out with remarkable rapidity. By

DAIMLER FLEETLINE
30 OR 33 FT. PASSENGER CHASSIS

that time West Riding had lost its independence. It had sold out to the Transport Holding Company for £1.9m in October 1967. Second-hand Lodekkas from other THC fleets – 77 in all, mostly elderly rear-entrance LDs – were drafted in to speed replacement of the Wulfrunians in 1969–70.

The 1966 Show also demonstrated the continuing interest in high-capacity single-deckers. While Daimler was showing a double-deck Fleetline for Leeds, on AEC's stand there was a Swift for Leeds with a 48-seat two-door Roe body. It was the first of an order for ten which would be the precursors of further larger batches of Leeds single-deckers.

One of the greatest exponents of one-man-operated standee buses at this time was Norman Morton, general manager of Sunderland Corporation, and in 1966 this undertaking received its last double-deckers, 12 Fleetlines, along with no fewer than 36 standee single-deckers. The bulk of these were Leyland Panthers, but there were also three Daimler Roadliners, one of which was at Earls Court. Morton developed a distinctive look for the town's new bus fleet with single-piece flat-glass windscreens and forward-sloping side pillars. Bodywork was by Strachans.

Sunderland's Panthers – which cost £6,600 each (compared with £6,814 for its 1965 Fleetlines) had the wheelbase reduced by 1ft to allow for a wider entrance door and their arrival heralded the introduction of a flat-fare of 4d on all the town's bus services. To try and speed loading, which Morton saw as crucial to the success of one-man-operated bus services, passengers were encouraged to buy tokens in

advance at the rate of 2s 9d for ten. The flat-fare scheme was replaced by zonal fares in 1969.

The intake of 36 single-deckers in one year meant that Sunderland was replacing 20 per cent of its fleet in one fell swoop. Another 54 single-deckers would follow in 1967–68 which meant that by the end of that year half of Sunderland's buses would be less than three years old.

Sunderland, incidentally, was the first British operator to run a two-door rear-engined double-decker, although not the first to order one. This came about through the

Willowbrook's first bodies on rear-engined chassis included six Atlanteans for Devon General in 1966 – one of the Loughborough builder's few double-deck orders from BET at this time. The other main users of this style of body were the municipal fleets at Cardiff, Coventry and Brighton. C. Aston

Sunderland Corporation, heavily influenced by operating practices on mainland Europe, embarked on an ambitious programme to convert the town's services to one-man-operation using single-deck buses and introducing a flat-fare. Most of the new buses were Leyland Panthers with bodies by Strachans to a design developed by Sunderland. Iain MacGregor

conversion in 1965 of a 12-month-old Fleetline which had been involved in an accident. The work was done with one-man-operation in mind, although it was not until July 1966 that double-deck one-man-operation was legalised, a change that was to reverse the trend towards single-deckers.

A few operators – including London Transport and Walsall Corporation – had considered using double-deckers as off-peak one-man buses by closing off the upper deck. Indeed the BET group had considered the possibility as early as 1961, but rejected it in the light of trade union opposition to single-deck omo. LT's Fleetlines had a partition which could be used to seal off the staircase and they were operated thus for a short period, while from 1965 Walsall's short Fleetlines were of two-door layout. The main door was still a sliding unit behind the front axle, but there was in addition a narrow entrance with a jack-knife door in the front overhang and the plan was that this would be used when the top deck was sealed off and the bus was being used for driver-only operation.

While rear-engined buses with the entrance opposite the driver were the obvious candidates for one-man-operation, some fleets did try running half-cabs without a conductor – a practice already accepted, mainly in rural areas, on single-deckers. Brighton was the first, having converted some forward-entrance PD2s which were in use as one-man buses within months of the double-deck omo legislation having come into effect. Brighton's last Titans, in 1968, were unusual among front-engined 'deckers in having been built as one-man buses.

Great Yarmouth Corporation was in fact the first operator of a double-decker without a conductor, having an Atlantean in service on 1 July 1966, albeit on a route aimed at holiday-makers and on which a flat fare was charged.

The first vehicles from either Bristol or ECW to be delivered to an operator outside the Tilling or Scottish groups as a result of the 1965 share exchange came from ECW and were five stylish dual-door bodies on Leyland Leopard L1s for West Hartlepool Corporation where they followed an earlier delivery of Strachans-bodied L1s. The body was generally similar to that fitted to the Bristol RE. They entered service at the start of 1967, albeit with 1966 D-suffix registrations.

They were soon followed by the first Bristols for municipal operation since 1950. These were six RESLs for Coventry Corporation and five for South Shields. All had ECW bodies. An essential factor in Bristol securing business from these and other municipal fleets was the availability of semi-automatic transmission on the RE, an option introduced just before the model became available on the open market.

The REs for South Shields were dual-door buses and they followed eleven Roe-bodied Fleetlines – which were the undertaking's last double-deckers and last Daimlers – delivered in 1965–66. The South Shields REs had curved windscreens which up to that time had been standard on RE bus bodies. Five similar buses (but with flat screens) in 1968 were South Shields' last new buses. The undertaking was absorbed by the new Tyneside PTE in January 1970.

Coventry's REs had a body with a new, more severe, front which had flat glass screens which allowed for a slightly wider entrance door. They were a mixture of both one- and two-door vehicles.

By the end of 1967 there were over 50 REs in municipal service, with Coventry, Hartlepool, Leicester, Luton, Newport, Reading, SHMD and South Shields – most of whom had previously been buying Daimlers or Leylands.

The deal struck between Leyland and Bristol/ECW saw the horizontal Leyland O.680 engine being offered as an option in the Bristol RE chassis – an option which was taken up by a number of Tilling companies

Brighton Corporation's last half-cabs were five Leyland Titan PD3/4s with 69-seat Metro-Cammell bodies. These entered service in 1968 – along with seven Panther Cubs – and were suitable for one-man-operation. David Brown

and also by some BET companies which ordered Bristols. Some operators experienced problems with the rear engine mountings on Leyland-powered RELL6L models. The mountings were prone to failure, which led to the rear end of the engine dropping on to the road. One of those operators was Ribble, and as a temporary expedient Ribble's early RELL6Ls were fitted with securing chains which, if the mountings failed, would keep the engine more or less in position and allow the defective bus to be driven slowly back to the depot. Stronger engine mountings ultimately cured the problem.

Other rear-engined single-deckers would soon be giving trouble too. On Leyland's Panther the weight

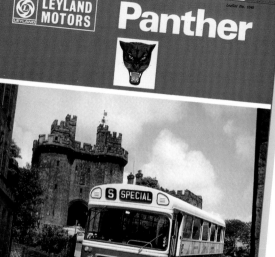

of the engine suspended in a relatively long rear overhang caused the chassis to flex. This in turn put pressure on the chassis outriggers – which could break – and on the body framing. Stronger outriggers were one solution, and body strengthening was common too, particularly at the rear. Bodies with generous pillar spacing were more likely to give trouble than those with more pillars and shorter bays. Similar problems affected other first-generation rear-engined single-deckers.

These buses, generally replacing half-cab

double-deckers, may have exuded modernity – but they lacked the reliability of the buses being replaced and often put a severe strain on operators' engineering departments.

Daimler, still promoting its Roadliner with vigour, clearly saw some virtue in developing the Fleetline as a single-decker, following the delivery of the batch to Birmingham in 1965. In 1966 it announced the SRG6. This was in effect the 18ft 6in wheelbase CRG6LX/33 double-deck chassis and was designed for bodywork up to 33ft long. In 1967 it would be offered with the option of longer front and rear overhangs to produce buses of 36ft overall length. The 33ft SRG6 had

In 1967 West Hartlepool was the first operator to receive ECW bodywork following the removal of restrictions on the sale of ECW bodies outside the state-owned sector of the bus industry. It took five, on Leyland Leopard L1 chassis.
Martin Llewellyn

Sales of the single-deck Fleetline were slow to start with but soon gathered pace, boosted in part by orders for Maidstone & District and Northern General and its associates. Sunderland District operated 17 36ft-long Fleetlines with Alexander W-type bodies. The use of short bays added strength to the body – but not enough to stop most 36ft Fleetlines from needing major remedial work to their bodies after a few years in service.
Chris Aston

Gardner's 122bhp 6LW engine as standard; while the 36ft model used the 150bhp 6LX. The 6LX could be had in the short model, while the 180bhp 6LXB was available for buyers of 36ft Fleetlines seeking more power.

The chassis frames were the same as on the CRG6 double-decker but with a strengthened rear section (although not strong enough, as operators would soon find out), smaller tyres and, on the 36ft version, a longer propeller shaft. The SRG6 was supplied without an engine cover, it being left to the bodybuilder to enclose the engine within the body. The first orders came from Grimsby-Cleethorpes and Halifax, both for 33ft models.

Meanwhile the Roadliner had won its biggest order – 50 for PMT. These comprised 24 with Plaxton bus bodies, 23 with Marshall bodies and three coaches. The first Plaxton-bodied bus was at the 1966 Commercial Motor Show and delivery of the remainder was spread throughout 1967. This was to be the best year for Roadliner bus deliveries with 83 entering service (out of a UK total of 134).

The Roadliner's Cummins V6 engine had been fitted experimentally to three double-deck Fleetlines – the original demonstrator, 7000HP, plus one bus at London Transport and another at North Western Road Car. In the autumn of 1966 Daimler indicated that the V6 would be available as an option on the Fleetline, but the rapidly-deteriorating reputation of the Cummins-powered Roadliner ensured that none were ordered.

Elsewhere among the municipalities, Aberdeen took its first Fleetlines, a natural progression from the CVG6s being delivered up to 1965. The Fleetlines cost £6,822 whereas the previous year's CVG6s had cost just £5,710 – a difference of 20 per cent. However carrying capacity was up too, so the cost per seat was little different – £87 for the CVG6s and £89 for the Fleetlines. The Fleetlines were accompanied by half-a-dozen Leyland Tiger Cubs with unusual two-door Alexander Y-type bodies (at a cost of £5,138 each) as Aberdeen tried one-man-operation. And while the Tiger Cubs were Aberdeen's first Leylands, joining a fleet of Daimler CVG6s and AEC Regents, it would be to Leyland that the corporation turned for double-deckers in 1967, with the delivery of 10 Atlanteans.

Down the North Sea coast in Dundee, Fleetlines had been introduced to the municipal bus fleet in 1964. Somewhat earlier – in November 1961 in fact – Dundee Corporation ordered 20 high-capacity single-deckers, AEC Reliances with 53-seat Alexander bodies, capable of carrying up to 24 standees. They were built in 1964 and delivered in 1965.

However Dundee had a history of militant trade unionism, and the Reliances were soon on their way back to Alexander, where they were stored until such times as agreement could be reached on their operation. They were finally registered and entered service – two years old but unused – in 1966.

Edinburgh Corporation was in transition in 1966, taking 50 new Leylands – a figure divided equally

LCT

Drivers' and Conductors' Handbook

ACCIDENTS

If an accident occurs, you must stop and give your name and address to any person who has reasonable grounds for asking for it.

An Accident Report on the proper form and signed by both the driver and the conductor, must be sent to Head Office as soon as possible.

Drivers must exchange names, addresses and registration numbers with the driver of any vehicle or any individual or owner of property, involved in an accident. If, for any reason, this instruction is not complied with, the accident must be reported to a Police Officer or at any Police Station within 24 hours of the occurrence. Where any personal injury is involved, the matter must always—whether or not names and addresses have been exchanged—be reported to the Police within 24 hours.

Bus Drivers are generally given by the Police a form instructing them to produce a Certificate of Insurance for inspection. State that the necessary document will be produced at Millgarth Street Police Station and pin the form you have received to your Accident Report. Head Office will then deal with the matter.

29

between Titans and Atlanteans. As before, the Titans had glass-fibre BMMO-style grilles and bonnets, produced at Edinburgh's Shrubhill central works. The PD3s were the city's last Titans – and they brought to almost 500 the number of Titans in Edinburgh service.

Elsewhere more operators were abandoning half-cab double-deckers. In Lancashire Ashton-under-Lyne switched from Titans to Atlanteans, taking its first PDR1s in 1966, while across the Pennines in Halifax the eight Titans which entered service were accompanied by seven Fleetlines. The Titans were Halifax's last; the Fleetline would become the undertaking's new standard. However the Titans were not quite the last half-cabs for Halifax. That distinction would go to five Dennis Lolines delivered in 1967. In nearby Huddersfield Daimler CVG6LX/30s entered service in 1966; from 1967 they would be succeeded by Fleetlines. Huddersfield, incidentally, had in 1964 taken six 27ft 6in-long CVG6LX models – unique high-powered short-wheelbase buses for the town's hilly routes.

Leeds had been ambivalent about engine locations. It had stuck with front-engined models – from AEC, Daimler and Leyland – until 1963. Fleetlines appeared in 1964 and Atlanteans in 1965 – accompanied by Regent Vs in both years – then in 1966 there were both Fleetlines and Atlanteans (in orders converted from CVG6/30s and Titan PD3s), still accompanied by Regent Vs. These were the last half-cabs for the fleet, but not the last AECs, as Leeds switched to one-man-operated AEC Swifts in a big way, building up a fleet of 120 by 1971 which made it the biggest user of Swifts outside London.

New types of buses required new driving techniques, not least because of their long front overhang. Leeds City Transport devoted seven pages of its Bus Drivers Handbook to its various rear-engined models. It warned, for example, that on Atlanteans and Fleetlines the distance from the driving seat to the nearside was "approximately one foot more than on the average bus" and that the front wheel track was six inches narrower than the rear. And on Atlanteans "a gear suitable to the road speed must be used to avoid transmission chatter associated with the self-lock flywheel". (Elsewhere the LCT drivers handbook included lists of hills and the gears to be selected at different points when descending them – lists which one suspects few drivers paid much attention to.)

In 1966 Derby received both front- and rear-engined Daimlers. The 12 CVG6s were really its 1965 fleet intake arriving late, and they were followed by 13 Fleetlines. All had Roe bodies, albeit of quite different styles – the classic teak-framed open-platform body on the CVG6s perhaps comparing unfavourably in passengers' eyes with the modernity offered by what might be described as a slightly softened version of the BET-inspired body fitted to the Fleetlines.

The last big batch of traditional front-engined buses for a Welsh fleet was delivered in 1966, with the arrival of 37 Guy Arab Vs in Cardiff. These had Alexander bodies and were a mix of 65-seat 28ft-long buses and 70-seat 30ft-long vehicles. Cardiff had a policy of accepting the lowest tender and had been buying Arabs, Regents and Titans. The 1966 Arabs would be its last. In 1967 it switched to Fleetlines.

Merthyr Tydfil also put its last half-cabs into service in 1966, five Leyland Titan PD3s with exposed radiators and forward-entrance East Lancs bodies. They were Merthyr's last double-deckers. From 1967 one-man-operated single-deckers – mainly Leyland Leopards with East Lancs bodies – would be Merthyr's choice.

Newport, which had last bought new double-deckers, PD2s, in 1961, introduced Alexander-bodied Leyland Atlanteans to its services in 1966. This became the fleet standard, with 42 in operation by 1971 making up just under half the fleet.

In 1967 Leyland revised its lowheight Atlantean chassis. The PDR1/2 had used a Daimler gearbox which had proved to be one of its weak points. This was addressed in its replacement, the PDR1/3, which had Leyland's own rationalised Pneumocyclic box. No PDR1/3s would be delivered until 1968 and PDR1/2s continued to enter service until the middle of 1967. Most had full-height bodywork, but buyers who opted for the PDR1/2 to take advantage of its low-height potential included BET companies East Midland, Ribble and Yorkshire Traction, and independents King Alfred of Winchester and South Yorkshire of Pontefract.

The BET PDR1/2s had bodies by Alexander and Northern Counties while the two independents specified near-identical Roe bodywork. For King Alfred they were the company's first rear-engined double-deckers, while South Yorkshire had previously bought PDR1/1s with lowbridge bodies. The last lowbridge Atlanteans entered service with Fishwick in 1966.

The only short Atlanteans were a trio of PDR1/2s for Great Yarmouth. These had 2ft taken out of the wheelbase to produce vehicles with an overall length of 28ft. They had 65-seat Roe bodies and entered service at the end of 1966.

The rationalised Pneumocyclic gearbox which featured in the PDR1/3 was also fitted to conventional Atlantean chassis which were designated PDR1A/1. The first entered service in the summer of 1968.

Daimler made changes to its Fleetline too, with the Mark 4A which had lower-geared

steering and some gearbox revisions. The revised steering was made standard on the 33ft-long Fleetline which, from 1968, was also available with power assistance.

By 1967 sales of AEC double-deckers were in steep decline. The last Renowns took to the road after a five-year production run. These were four for City of Oxford and one for Leigh. Renown production had totalled just 251, a lower figure even than the competing Lowlander. And sales of Regent Vs were down too. Just 52 entered service in 1967. The biggest deliveries were to Southampton (22) and East Kent (15). Southampton had been buying Regent Vs since 1962; East Kent since 1958. Southampton would switch to the Atlantean in 1968; East Kent to the Fleetline in 1969 – although in East Kent's case with substantial numbers of AEC Swift single-deckers too.

Guy Arab deliveries actually outnumbered AEC Regents in 1967, although this was to be the last year when significant numbers of new Guys would take to Britain's streets. The reason was two large orders: 31 for Wolverhampton and 26 for Lancashire United. All were 30ft-long forward-entrance buses. Those for Lancashire United had Northern Counties bodies and would be long-lived. Wolverhampton's had Strachans bodies – that manufacturer's last and biggest postwar double-deck contract – which proved to be less than satisfactory. None were recertified for further service after their initial seven year

Certificates of Fitness expired, and most were in fact sold for scrap in 1973 by the West Midlands PTE which had absorbed Wolverhampton Corporation's bus operations in 1969.

Daimler's Fleetline was enjoying growing success – a record 476 entered service in 1967, compared with 373 Atlanteans, but sales of front-engined models were down to single figures – five CVG6s for Northampton and three CVG6/30s for Swindon.

The Dennis Loline reached the end of the road in 1967 with the delivery of five to Halifax, and so too did the Albion Lowlander. The last went to South Notts, the only independent to buy Lowlanders, and brought its fleet of the type to five. All had Northern Counties bodies and were LR3s with manual gearboxes. From 1968 South Notts would buy lowheight Atlantean PDR1/3s. Leyland had in total sold fewer Lowlanders than even its most conservative market forecasts had predicted – the final total was 274 – and it was left with stocks of unwanted chassis side-members on its hands.

Production of the Bristol Lodekka for the Tilling and Scottish groups was continuing at a reasonably high level with 401 being delivered in 1966, a figure which fell to 287 in 1967 but maintained the Lodekka as Britain's best-selling front-engined double-decker, a position it had occupied since 1962 by dint of the conservative operating policies of the two state-owned bus operating groups. The last of the short rear-entrance FS series models were delivered in 1966 with sizeable batches going to Crosville (35), United Counties (21) and West Yorkshire (33). Five for Lincolnshire Road Car were the last Lodekkas to be fitted with five-cylinder Gardner engines. In 1967 all Lodekkas were FLF models, including some with an extended rear overhang which took the overall length up to 31ft and increased the seating capacity from 70 to a maximum of 78.

Long FLFs were delivered to SBG companies Alexander (Fife) and Central SMT in 1967, and brought to and end deliveries of Lodekkas to Scotland. Of the other SBG companies which had been buying Lodekkas, Western SMT had switched to Fleetlines in 1965, and Alexander (Midland) followed in 1967.

Production of Bristol engines was being wound down in 1966 and finally ceased in 1967, with the last being fitted to FLFs for Bristol Omnibus, Hants & Dorset, United Auto, United Counties and Wilts & Dorset. At the same time as receiving the last FLF6B models, the associated Hants & Dorset and Wilts & Dorset fleets received 16 FLF6Ls – the only Lodekkas to be built with Leyland engines apart from a few FLFs delivered to Bristol and Cumberland in 1963 which were fitted with O.600 engines as an experiment. The 1967 FLF6L chassis was one of the more unusual side effects of the share exchange between Leyland and Bristol.

Another relatively late change to the FLF was the option of semi-automatic or automatic transmission. Although no orders were placed for the latter, almost half of the 219 FLFs ordered by THC in its 1966–67 programme had semi-automatic gearboxes.

The pursuit of high capacity saw Western

SMT take delivery of Scotland's first 33ft-long double-deckers in 1967. These were six Fleetlines with 83-seat Northern Counties bodies, giving them the highest seating capacity of any bus then in service in Britain. A sixth long Fleetline for Western, but with Alexander body, was an exhibit at the 1967 Scottish Motor Show. All were crew-operated on Paisley local services. Subsequent SBG Fleetlines reverted to the more common nominal 30ft overall length with 75 seats.

Also at the Scottish show was a 33ft-long Atlantean for Edinburgh Corporation. It had an 82-seat Alexander body with panoramic windows and before entering service in Edinburgh in the spring of 1968 was demonstrated to Newcastle Corporation. It remained unique; subsequent Edinburgh Atlanteans were standard-wheelbase PDR1A/1s.

The move to bigger double-deckers would gain some momentum, but was far from universal. Instead operators were still looking at high-capacity single-deckers.

Manchester, for example, with a predominantly double-deck fleet, put 29 Metro-Cammell-bodied Panthers into service in 1967. There should have been 30, but one was destroyed by a fire at Metro-Cammell and was not replaced. These were 40-seaters capable of carrying 20 standing passengers and were, of course, one-man-operated. To reduce boarding times the services on which they operated had a simplified fares structure – 6d, 1s, 1s 6d –

and the buses had Bell Punch Autoslot coin-in-the-slot ticket machines linked to turnstiles. The turnstiles were unreliable and were quickly abandoned. The Autoslot machines didn't work too well, and were replaced by Johnson fare-boxes.

The Panthers weren't that wonderful either. The bodies had to be strengthened after five years, and none lasted in Manchester beyond the expiry of their initial Certificates of Fitness in 1974.

Lincoln Corporation turned to Panthers in 1967, uniquely putting into service that year both old-style exposed-radiator Titans and new-generation rear-engined Panthers. The Titans, which followed earlier deliveries of Atlanteans, were to be Lincoln's last double-deckers until the mid-1970s. By 1970 Lincoln would be running 25 Panthers, all with single-doorway Roe bodywork.

The short-lived Panther Cub was chosen by Portsmouth, and it put 26 into service in 1967 with the body order divided between Marshall and Metro-Cammell. Further along the south coast Brighton Corporation bought seven which joined its all-double-deck fleet but withdrew them after seven years. As with many other operators Brighton felt they were not really suited for arduous urban operation; they were prone to overheating on the town's hilly routes. Typically Panther Cubs lasted no more then 10 years – a short life by the standards of most operators.

While Daimler was actively promoting its Fleetline as a single-decker, Leyland did not do the same with the Atlantean. However in 1967 Great Yarmouth Corporation, which had bought short Atlantean double-deckers in 1966, ordered three Atlanteans to be fitted with Marshall single-deck bodies. These seated just 31 and were remarkably similar to the Fleetlines built for Birmingham 1965, but with side fairings over the engine to disguise the fact that it protruded from the rear of the body.

Birmingham, meanwhile, had decided to try AEC Swifts, taking 18 with Metro-Cammell bodies (and a mixture of AH505 and AH691 engines) in 1967. The order followed trials of a Swift, an RELL6G, a Panther and a Roadliner. They replaced double-deckers on

Lincoln's last double-deckers for some years were four Leyland Titan PD2s in 1967. These had 62-seat Roe bodies and were among the last forward-entrance bodies to be built by the Leeds-based coachbuilder. They served Lincoln for 10 years, a relatively short life which reflected the growing move towards one-man-operation in the 1970s – a role for which most operators accepted half-cab 'deckers were ill-suited. Iain MacGregor

city routes but were not deemed a success and in 1969 the services reverted to double-deck operation. The Swifts then moved on to traditional single-deck services, replacing elderly Leyland Tiger PS2s in 1969.

Not all operators contemplating high-capacity single-deckers were looking at complex rear-engined models. SBG had in 1964 discovered the 36ft Leopard bus. Fitted with an Alexander Y-type 53-seat body which was licensed to carry 24 standing passengers, it could be used to replace 53-seat lowbridge double-deckers dating from the late 1940s. Central SMT at this time ran some 650 vehicles of which just 30 were single-deck buses. In 1964–65 it had put a small number of 53-seat Leopards into service – 19 – but in the period 1967–69 they would be joined by a further 70, marking a major move away from double-deck operation which would continue through the 1970s.

The big plus-point of the Leopard was its simplicity – a proven engine coupled to a straightforward drive train and all mounted in a strong, trouble-free, chassis. SBG's Leopards at this stage all had Leyland's four-speed manual gearbox. The downside of all

this was a three-step entrance and a narrow doorway, but as a trade-off for in-service reliability and low running costs this was something Central SMT and other SBG companies were prepared to live with. Low weight – just under 7 tons on early Y-type Leopards, contributed to good fuel economy.

Various double-deck types were disappearing from major fleets during the 1960s. The Albion Venturer, rare outside its native city, disappeared from the Glasgow Corporation fleet in 1963, with the withdrawal of buses which were just ten years old. That they were the only buses in the fleet with manual gearboxes must have hastened their demise. Few Venturers survived anywhere beyond the middle of the decade. Crossleys, which had been considerably more numerous, fared rather better. Manchester's and Stockport's Crossleys reached the end of the road in 1967, Birmingham's last was taken out of service in 1969. Among other major Crossley buyers Bolton had disposed of its by 1962, Liverpool's had all gone by 1963, while Rotherham's – which had been the last to enter service – lasted until 1969. Foden double-deckers, even less common than Albion's Venturer,

vanished from the fleets of the two major users, Chester and Warrington, in 1970 and 1972 respectively.

Changes were taking place in the structure of the bus operating industry and in November 1967 BET announced that it was selling its UK bus operations to the state-owned Transport Holding Company. BET ran around 11,000 vehicles, compared with 10,000 in the THC companies. The sale – for £35m – took effect from March 1968. The THC had controlled all of what were still generally known as the Tilling group bus companies since 1963 when it had taken over from the British Transport Commission. Ownership of 75 per cent of Bristol and ECW was also vested in the THC.

This meant that all of the major bus operations in England and Wales outside London were either under THC control or were municipally-operated with the notable exception of independents Lancashire United Transport which ran 400 vehicles, and Barton Transport with 330. Most other independents ran fleets of fewer than 50 buses.

1968-69

THOSE WERE THE DAYS

THE BIG event of 1968, and one which shaped the future of Britain's bus manufacturing industry, was the merger of the Leyland Motor Corporation with British Motor Holdings to create the British Leyland Motor Corporation – an organisation which in the 1970s would be the butt of many comedians' jokes. The move was motivated primarily by the government's desire to strengthen Britain's car industry, but it brought together Leyland and AEC with BMH-owned rivals Daimler and Guy. Add to that Leyland's 25 per cent stake in Bristol and ECW, and you had the makings of a monolithic bus builder.

In 1968 the tide had finally turned against front-engined double-deckers. Just 168 were delivered – out of a total of only 1,123 new double-deckers entering UK service. This was in itself a record low figure, depressed by the continuing interest in standee single-deckers. Deliveries of rear-engined single-deck buses hit a high in 1968 of nearly 1,250, a figure boosted by almost 400 Merlins for London Transport.

There were no new front-engined buses for either BET or SBG. Tilling group companies took just 71 FLF Lodekkas, including some of the extra-long variant for Eastern National. With the last of the Lodekkas – after a produc-

tion run of over 5,200 – came the end of the lowheight front-engined double-decker. The Lodekka's success makes the attempts of AEC, Dennis and Leyland to promote lowheight double-deckers look pretty poor. AEC did best, but sold just 431, made up of 180 Bridgemasters and 251 Renowns. Next came Dennis with 280 Lolines. And last came Leyland which sold 274 Lowlanders.

Only ten double-deckers entered London Transport service in 1968. These were the last Routemasters. LT's attention was firmly focused on AEC Merlins.

Among the traditional small independents, never big buyers of new double-deckers,

Garelochhead Coach Services bought an AEC Regent V – Scotland's last new half-cab – while Harper of Heath Hayes bought three Leyland Titan PD3s, which were the last half-cabs for an English independent. The Garelochhead bus was the last Regent to be powered by AEC's AV470 engine, an option which had been popular in the 1950s, but which from the early 1960s became relatively rare as most fleets opted for the bigger AV590.

The remaining half-cabs were for municipal fleets, and for most they were to be the last. On the Isle of Man, Douglas Corporation took two Regent Vs, the last chassis to be built (although not the last to enter service), and the last double-deckers for Douglas.

The last home-market front-engined Daimlers entered service in 1968. These were three CCG5s with rear-entrance Massey bodies for Burton-on-Trent, and five Roe-bodied CVG6s for Northampton Corporation. The three Burton Daimlers brought to 21 the number of crash-gearbox CCG5s in the fleet. They were the last buses built with Gardner 5LW engines. To Northampton went the distinction of putting into service the UK's last open-platform double-deckers in October 1968.

Leyland Titans were delivered to Bedwas & Machen, Blackpool, Bradford, Brighton, Darwen, Leicester, Stockport and Wigan. Darwen and Stockport would receive more in 1969, but for the other fleets they marked the end of an era. The numbers might have been falling, but the variety remained with a mixture of both exposed radiators and St Helens fronts, PD2s and PD3s, and forward- and rear-entrance bodies.

The Titan for Bedwas & Machen was an exposed-radiator PD3 and it had the last side-gangway lowbridge body to be built. This was by Massey. The production of lowbridge bodywork on front-engined chassis had dropped dramatically after 1961 when the Scottish group switched from Leyland Titans to Albion Lowlanders. The last built for

service in England had been two Massey-bodied Guy Arab Vs in 1963. These had been ordered by Moore of Kelvedon but were delivered to Eastern National who had taken over the Moore business at the start of 1963. Unusually for 30ft-long buses they had Gardner 5LW engines.

Massey, incidentally, had been taken over by Northern Counties in 1967. Both companies were based in Wigan. Northern Counties was building on average around 120 bodies a year, compared with just 45 – one a week – at Massey. The vehicles for Burton-on-Trent and Bedwas & Machen marked the end of ten years of production of Massey's classic body for front-engined chassis. The company's body for Atlanteans and Fleetlines was rather less graceful and only 32 were built. These were on Atlanteans for Maidstone (20), Colchester (10) and A1 Service of Ardrossan (one), and on a solitary Fleetline for A1.

So in 1968 the bulk of Britain's new double-deck buses were either Daimler Fleetlines – a record 540 – or Leyland Atlanteans. The fall in sales of front-engined double-deckers was given a final push by the Labour government of the day. Bus operators throughout Britain were struggling on two counts. Firstly, fewer and fewer people were travelling by bus. Bus use had peaked in the early 1950s and had been declining steadily ever since in the face of changing social patterns – in particular rising car ownership and the spread of television (which also had a drastic effect on cinema attendance). The number of cars on Britain's roads more than doubled between 1955 and 1965. And in most

Brighton Corporation's first motorbuses, in 1939, were 21 AEC Regents. These were joined after the war by 14 Regent IIIs which had 56-seat Weymann bodies. These handsome buses would serve the town for almost 20 years, with the last being replaced by Leyland Panther Cubs delivered in 1968 and suitable for one-man-operation. The 20-year life of the Regents contrasted sharply with the seven years achieved by the Panther Cubs. The comparison highlights some of the problems the industry faced in adopting new types of vehicles. David Brown

parts of the country there was a perpetual shortage of drivers and conductors.

One answer to falling revenues and shortages of staff, as bus operators themselves were well aware, was to make greater use of one-man buses even though this often met resistance from the trades unions involved – for most operators this being the Transport & General Workers Union.

To encourage operators to extend one-man operation, the Government introduced in 1968 a system of capital grants towards the purchase of new buses. This followed a transport white paper in 1967 which recog-

nised the industry's problems and said: "The rapid extension of one-man operation of buses is essential to hold down costs of operation in the face of rising costs and the fall in passengers. If one-man operation is to be introduced as quickly as it should be, this will require the replacement – earlier than customary – of existing buses not suitable for such operation."

The grant scheme set out a range of criteria including some key dimensions, and, of course, stipulated that the bus had to be suitable for one-man operation. Front-engined double-deckers were excluded from the list of approved layouts eligible for what was generally known as the New Bus Grant. And that accelerated the type's demise.

The grant started as 25 per cent of the purchase price. In 1971 this was increased to 50 per cent. It was a major boost to fleet replacement programmes, although some operators looked this particular gift horse in the mouth. The Scottish Bus Group in its review of 1969 grumbled that: "It is a sad fact, however, now becoming increasingly evident, that all the sophistications of modern vehicles

now demanded, such as power doors, greater heating, larger engines and consequently brakes – all adopted by the Ministry of Transport in its 'standardisation' concept – are materially adding to operating costs." They might have added: "Bring back the Leyland Titan!"

Lancashire United Transport said much the same with chairman Sir Robert Cary regretting the company's need to buy double-deckers "of a type which would be more costly to purchase, more costly to run and less suitable for its requirements".

While the switch to one-man operation did save the wages of a conductor, omo drivers were paid a premium rate which was typically in the order of 15 per cent on a single-decker and 20 per cent on a double-decker, although these figures could be as high as 22.5 and 25 per cent respectively in some of the bigger urban operations. At this premium – and with the possibility of increased running time and perhaps even the need for an extra bus on the route – the financial benefits of omo were in danger of being eroded.

By now the number of newcomers to rear-engined double-deck models was slowing down. Blackburn, the Tees-side Railless Traction Board and Wigan switched from Titans to Atlanteans, Blackburn getting the first of the revised PDR1A/1 models, with locally-manufactured East Lancs bodies. Ipswich and Southampton had been buying AEC Regents; both switched to Atlanteans. Those for Ipswich were of interest in that they had bodywork by ECW – along with similar buses for Leicester they were the first Atlanteans to have ECW bodywork. Swindon

took its first Fleetlines – a natural progression from the CVG6/30s of the previous year.

Now that one-man-operation of double-deckers was permitted, a number of urban operators were looking at the use of two-doors on 'deckers. Newcastle Corporation's 1968 Atlanteans had dual-door Alexander bodies, as did its 1969 delivery, the first of which was in the demonstration park at the 1968 Earls Court show. This differed from previous Atlanteans for Newcastle (or anywhere else, for that matter) by having a forward-ascending nearside staircase. The idea was to provide easier access to the exit (the staircase was located behind the nearside front wheel) and reduce congestion in the area between the entrance and the foot of the staircase which was perceived as a problem with conventional offside stairs. The new layout cost Newcastle five seats, but it became a standard for the Tyneside PTE which took over from the Corporation at the start of 1970.

The rear-engined double-decker had been around for nearly ten years and body designs had been gradually improving, bringing more style to urban buses. The leaders had been two of the big municipal fleets, Glasgow and Liverpool, while Bolton and Sunderland, too, had done some pioneering work. Elsewhere designs had been tweaked – in Manchester, for example, where from 1965 the Metro-Cammell bodies fitted to Atlanteans and Fleetlines had curved windscreens and a front panel with a broad horizontal moulding. Metro-Cammell also supplied this style of front to Cardiff, Plymouth and Salford corporations, and to BET company Devon General.

It was in Manchester that double-deck

The Earls Court exhibition hall in London, site of the 1968 Commercial Motor Show, provides a backdrop for a Newcastle Corporation Leyland Atlantean with Alexander body. The use of two doors on double-deckers enjoyed brief but fairly widespread popularity among urban fleets, although most soon abandoned the concept. Newcastle was unique in specifying a nearside staircase on its Atlanteans, hence the solid panel ahead of the exit door. The illuminated Pay on Entry sign below the Atlantean badge was a common fixture in the early days of one-man-operation and could be switched off if the vehicle was carrying a conductor. The British Leyland badge below was affixed purely for the Earls Court show. *Harry Hay*

It didn't take a lot to improve the appearance of an Atlantean as these two Plymouth Corporation buses show. The 1964 bus on the left has Metro-Cammell bodywork of the style which had been that builder's standard since the first production Atlanteans in 1958, while the 1967 vehicle alongside shows an alternative frontal treatment which was first seen on Manchester Corporation buses in 1964. Note the more modern fleet number transfer on the newer bus. *Geoff Rixon*

The Mancunian was one of the most striking designs of the 1960s, with its big side windows and deep windscreens. Developed by Manchester Corporation and built initially by Park Royal, it was the first double-decker to be purpose-designed for driver-only operation. It was built on Atlantean and Fleetline chassis. This is a Fleetline. Alan Mortimer

design was about to take a giant leap forward. Ralph Bennett, who had done much to make Bolton's Atlanteans look interesting, had in 1965 moved from the managership of Bolton to that of Manchester. Bennett, working with Ken Mortimer, a designer on Manchester Corporation's staff, and with bodybuilder Park Royal, produced a radical new look for the bodies on 48 Atlanteans and 48 Fleetlines delivered in 1968. The Fleetline chassis were, incidentally, more expensive than the Atlanteans – £3,569 against £3,327, an on-cost of just over 7 per cent. However it could be argued that lower fuel bills for the Gardner-powered Fleetlines would go a long way to cancelling out their higher initial cost.

The new style was christened the Mancunian and it marked a complete break from all that had gone before. It had big side windows – the same depth on both decks – and a deep curved windscreen. The side pillar spacing on the Mancunians was 6ft 6in at a time when most bodybuilders were standardised on a figure of 3ft 11in. The design was uncompromisingly angular, but its proportions and a bright livery layout gave it a crisp appearance which set the shape of things to come.

The Mancunians were two-door 73-seaters with two-step entrances and were the first purpose-designed one-man-operated double-deckers in Britain, and the first new dual-door 'deckers to enter service. They were licensed to carry up to 23 standees. The staircase was located opposite the centre exit. The first entered service in April 1968, and one was displayed by Park Royal at the Commercial Motor Show later that year.

While Manchester was embracing one-man-operated double-deckers, Liverpool Corporation had changed an order for Atlanteans to one for Panthers, taking 110, delivery of which started in the summer of 1968 and continued into the spring of 1969. These had Metro-Cammell bodies, two-door of course, and were 47-seaters with room for 24 standees. The bodies were of unusual appearance. To minimise the number of different sizes of glass being used, all the main side windows were the same size – not unusual in itself, but slightly odd when the window line had to be stepped because of the higher floor level at the rear.

They introduced a bright livery which used cream as the main body colour, with green restricted to the area around the windows and applied in a way which helped disguise the stepped waist. The cream-based livery was intended to distinguish one-man buses and was applied to a couple of Atlanteans until it was realised that the logical outcome of this policy would be a fleet of buses in cream rather than the established green. When the Panthers came up for repaint the livery was reversed to the traditional green and cream, rather than cream and green. And the Panthers marked the abandonment of Liverpool's use of fleet numbers with prefix letters to differentiate between makes of chassis. This was Leyland's biggest single order for Panthers.

Cardiff, which had bought its first rear-engined double-deckers – Fleetlines – in 1967 standardised on the type, although with a range of bodies: Metro-Cammell, Park Royal and Willowbrook. However in 1968 it bought a batch of 20 AEC Swifts with two-door Alexander W-type bodies with a simplified front end incorporating flat glass screens and a plain front panel. These were to introduce one-man-operation to the city which they did, although not until 1970 when agreement was finally reached with the trade union. Until then they ran with conductors.

Belfast Corporation, which was running 181 Fleetline double-deckers, took delivery of 36 single-deckers in 1969 – 18 Swifts and 18 Roadliners. Here, too, union resistance delayed their entry into service until early 1970.

It wasn't only the big urban fleets which had to deal with recalcitrant unions. Tilling-owned Thames Valley bought eight Bristol RESLs with dual-door ECW bodies in the autumn of 1967. They were 38-seaters licensed to carry up to 27 standees and were to bring one-man-operation to the company's services in Reading, following Reading Corporation's lead. The union objected and the buses were finally put into service in the spring of 1968, upseated to 40 with the standard figure of eight standing passengers – and any ideas of high standee loads abandoned. This reduced their carrying capacity dramatically – from a planned 65 to an actual 48.

Rear-engined single-deckers – AEC Swifts, Daimler Roadliners and Leyland Panthers – were still being delivered to BET fleets. Unusual among these were 30 Panthers for Maidstone & District which were bodied by Strachans and marked that builder's only significant order from BET. Like so many single-deck bodies of the time they weren't quite up to the flexing created by the heavy rear-mounted engine and all had to be rebuilt by either Willowbrook or ECW when they were just five years old. Maidstone & District was, incidentally, the second-biggest UK

Panther operator after Liverpool, with 95 entering service between 1965 and 1968.

Also noteworthy was a Panther for Northern General, which was exhibited at the 1968 Commercial Motor Show. This had a new Marshall Camair body, with a deep cantrail which was glazed on the nearside but panelled over on the offside, where there was a luggage rack above the windows. The aim was to give standing passengers a better view out. The interior was striking too, with polished plastic seat backs and a 1960s Pop-Art flowery pattern around the concealed fluorescent lighting which ran the full length of the bus down the centre of the ceiling. The interior styling – described as Northern Rose – was by John and Sylvia Reid who also played a part in the Park Royal Royalist coach body of the same period. A promotional leaflet posed the question: "Why shouldn't a bus be gay and colourful inside?"

The show Panther was the fore-runner of 25 which were divided between Northern General (18), Gateshead & District (three), Tyneside Omnibus Co (two, the company's first ever single-deckers) and Sunderland District (two). The Camair Panthers followed a prototype Camair Leopard delivered to Northern General in 1967.

One of PMT's fleet of Roadliners was destroyed by fire in 1969 but was considered worth rebodying, a job done by Plaxton, who were bodying ten new Roadliners for PMT at the time. However by 1972 attitudes had changed and PMT had started withdrawing Roadliners which were only five years old. The rebodied bus did no better than the rest and was sold in 1973 – for scrap.

The Cummins V6 engine in the Roadliner was faring badly. One problem was over-heating and if this was not recognised by the driver it would reach the point where the build up of pressure in the cooling system would force the filler cap off, sending a spout of steam and scalding water high into the air. The Roadliner's drivetrain layout restricted Daimler to the use of a compact engine and for an alternative to the Cummins it turned to Perkins, offering a V8 unit as an option from late 1968. In this configuration the Roadliner became the SRP8. The only SRP8 buses were a demonstrator and ten for PMT, delivered in 1969. All had Plaxton bodies.

The availability of a 36ft-long Fleetline single-decker may have been tacit admission by Daimler that they had got it wrong with the Roadliner, and at the 1968 Commercial Motor Show there was a demonstrator with two-door Alexander W-type body in Dundee Corporation colours. Major orders for the SRG6/36 came from Leeds (30), Maidstone & District (30), Belfast Corporation (30) and Dundee Corporation (25). The Leeds buses were unique at that time in having the more powerful Gardner 6LXB engine in place of the standard 6LX.

Long double-deckers started to appear in quantity during 1968, mainly in busy municipal fleets. Leeds put sixty 33ft-long Fleetlines and Atlanteans into operation. These had Roe and Park Royal bodies with the last 15 being of dual-door layout. To the south, Sheffield also switched to long buses, taking 30 PDR2/1s with two-door 79-seat Park Royal bodies and by 1970 would be running almost 200.

The Park Royal bodies for Sheffield were of a striking new design with longer bays and deep windows on both decks. These were neither as long nor as deep as the windows on the Mancunian, but they were a marked improvement on previous designs of Park Royal bodies on rear-engined chassis. The initial design had peaked domes and shallow windscreens – features which would disappear in the following years.

The Roadliner was one of the least successful designs of the 1960s, thanks in part to the unreliability of the Cummins V6 engine. Eastbourne Corporation operated three Roadliners with East Lancs bodies. Martin Llewellyn

Double-deck bodywork was undergoing change in the late 1960s, with Park Royal and the associated Roe business switching from five-bay to four-bay construction and adopting equal depth windows on both decks. The result was a considerable improvement, as shown by East Kent's first rear-engined double-deckers, which were 20 Fleetlines delivered in 1969. These were also the first Gardner-engined buses for East Kent since the last of the Guy Arabs in 1957; in the intervening years all of East Kent's new full-sized buses had been AECs. David Brown

The first 33ft double-decker for an independent was delivered to A1 of Ardrossan towards the end of 1968. It was a PDR2/1 Atlantean with Sheffield-style two-door Park Royal body.

Since the entry into service of the two Bristol VRLs in 1966 work had been going on at Bristol in developing the design further. The outcome was a rethink which saw the longitudinal engine layout being abandoned and in its place a transverse Gardner 6LX engine being fitted. This reduced the rear overhang. Thus was born the VRT, with a mechanical layout broadly similar to that used by the established Atlantean and Fleetline models. The ECW body was similar to that fitted to the VRLs, but with a different windscreen layout (which still used flat glass) while the overall length of the most common variant was 30ft 5in, compared with just over 33ft for VRLs.

The VRL survived for a short time. Twenty-five were exported to South Africa in 1969 and production continued until 1972 of chassis for use as motorway express coaches by Standerwick, which built up a fleet of 30 such vehicles.

When the VRT was announced in mid 1967 Bristol intended to offer a range of engines, including the Leyland O.600 and O.680 and AEC AV691 – the last-named tantalisingly offering AEC users the chance to buy a rear-engined double-decker. However none of these options made it into production. An unusual feature of the VRT was a choice of frame heights – either 18in or 21in. The VRT was one of the first British bus chassis to feature an air-operated handbrake, rather than the conventional manually-operated pull-on type.

Two VRTs entered service with Thames Valley at the end of 1968, while 25 were delivered to Scottish Omnibuses. The Scottish vehicles were 18ft 6in wheelbase VRT/LL (Long, Low) models – 32ft 9in long with 82-seat ECW bodies. They were the only VRT/LL models to be bodied by ECW. Those for Thames Valley were the more common VRT/SL (Short, Low) model with a 16ft 2in wheelbase, an overall length of 30ft 5in and an ECW body with 70 seats. The Tilling companies were less concerned than others about squeezing in the maximum number of seats – so initial deliveries of VRTs seated the same number of people as an FLF Lodekka.

Deliveries of Bristol VRTs shot up to 213 in 1969 – although it would be 1973 before they crossed the 200 mark again. The biggest buyers of VRTs in 1969 were West Yorkshire, with 49, followed by Eastern Counties (25) and United Auto (21). But one major buyer of Lodekkas, Crosville, avoided the new model and instead started buying large numbers of rear-engined single-deckers.

With the switch from the Lodekka to the VRT there came a fuel consumption penalty. Western National's FLF6Gs were averaging 12.1mpg – the figure for its VRTs was 9.85, although they were being used on busier routes and had semi-automatic transmissions while the Lodekkas had manual gearboxes.

The first municipal order for the Bristol VRT came from an unlikely source – Leyland-oriented Liverpool Corporation. Liverpool ordered 25 high-frame long-wheelbase VRT/LH models, which were the first VRTs with power-assisted steering, an item of specification which could be seen as reflecting the tougher stance taken by urban municipal crews than by drivers working for company operators. They were also the first new Liverpool buses to be powered by Gardner engines since a small batch of wartime Guys. And they were the first VRTs to be bodied by a builder other than ECW – East Lancs. They were delivered to the Merseyside PTE in 1970, which became the only user of high-frame VRTs.

The unconventional layout of the VRL attracted the attention of an unconventional municipal manager, R Edgley Cox at Walsall. He had been buying short Fleetlines, and at the 1968 Commercial Motor Show there was on display Britain's first 36ft-long two-axle double-deck bus. This was based on a Daimler CRC6/36 chassis, and while two-axle 36ft-long double-deckers had been permissible since 1961, it was an increase in the gross vehicle weight from 14 to 16 tons in 1964 which made the concept one worth trying.

The CRC6/36 had an 18ft 6in wheelbase and was powered by a Cummins V6 engine mounted VRL-style in the rear offside corner and driving straight to the rear axle, eliminating the angle drive of the standard Fleetline. The angle drive in the Fleetline reversed the rotation of the engine and in its place was fitted a reversing box. The Cummins V6 was rated at 200bhp, making this the most powerful double-deck bus yet seen in Britain. Daimler offered a choice of Daimatic or Allison gearboxes – Walsall opted for the semi-automatic Daimatic. The frame was swept out at the offside rear to hold the engine. The radiator was mounted at the front.

The Show bus had a low-height dual-door Northern Counties body, with the second door in the rear overhang. It had two staircases (the one at the rear ascending over the engine). A television monitor in the driving compartment – and remember this is 1968 – allowed the driver to watch the rear platform area. Walsall's CRC6/36 set a new record for seating capacity: 86. It was also one of the last buses to be built with an illuminated exterior advertising panel on the offside. This was fitted lower than normal, just above the lower deck windows, and was flush with the body side – whereas those used earlier in the decade had stood proud of the body. It was lit by the fluorescent tubes which provided interior lighting for the lower saloon.

The CRC6/36 proved to be a blind alley. Walsall's was the only one to enter UK service. The only other sales were 16 to Johannesburg Municipal Transport, which had been instrumental in its development, and where they ran alongside Bristol VRLs. The Walsall bus was designed for one-man operation, but was in fact always crew-operated both by Walsall and by the West Midlands PTE which succeeded it. West Midlands withdrew it in 1974, although it did find further service with a succession of small operators.

By 1969 Glasgow had 500 Atlanteans in service (more than any other operator at this time). It had been experimenting, rather half-heartedly, with one-man operated single-deckers. Its first Alexander-bodied Panther had been at the 1964 Commercial Motor Show. A second was at the 1965 Scottish Motor Show. And a third appeared at the 1967 Scottish show, differing from the first two by

having panoramic windows. Glasgow then ordered 13 – hardly an auspicious number – which entered service in 1969. The three original Panthers, all of which had Voith gearboxes, were withdrawn in 1971. The remaining 13 had considerably shorter lives than most Glasgow buses.

Blackpool Corporation's last Leyland PD3s were delivered in 1968 at which time its bus fleet was made up entirely of Titans. But for 1969 it ordered 15 AEC Swifts with dual-door Marshall bodies and these became the fleet standard. The order was originally going to be for Leyland Panthers – but the Swifts were cheaper. Swifts were also favoured by St Helens from 1968 with 44-seat-plus-20 standing Marshall bodies.

A rather smaller municipal fleet – running just 15 buses – which switched from open-platform double-deckers to two-door Swifts was Lowestoft. The availability of ECW bodywork on the open market allowed Lowestoft to support its local coachbuilder, and in 1969 it took four Swifts with 50-seat ECW bodies. By 1973 it would have ten.

Britain's last half-cab double-deckers entered service in 1969, and there were just 25 of them. Leading the field was, appropriately, the Leyland Titan which had been a consistent best-seller over the years. The last PD2 Titans were three for Darwen, with St Helens fronts and forward-entrance East Lancs bodies which were unusual among half-cabs in being

built from the outset for one-man-operation. And there were 14 PD3s, all with old-fashioned looking exposed radiators. Twelve went to Stockport and two to Ramsbottom. Ramsbottom's last PD3, with forward-entrance East Lancs body, was in fact delivered to the newly-created SELNEC (South East Lancashire North East Cheshire) PTE in November, although in full Ramsbottom livery. It was the very last half-cab bus to enter UK service.

In the interests of component standardisation, the final Titans incorporated some parts which were common to the Atlantean, now running at much higher levels of production than the Titan. This brought about a new series of type codes in which the A suffix indicated a chassis with Leyland's rationalised Pneumocyclic gearbox, rather than the fitment of a St Helens-style bonnet.

The other 1969 half-cabs were two Willowbrook-bodied AEC Regent Vs for Pontypridd, and six Guy Arab Vs for Chester. For both manufacturers they were the last double-deckers to enter UK service. Chester

Left **West Riding was purchased by the THC in 1967. To replace the company's troublesome Guy Wulfrunians a fleet of 75 second-hand Bristol Lodekkas were moved to West Riding from elsewhere in the Tilling group in 1969–70. These included LD6G models which were almost ten years older than some of the buses they were replacing. This bus came from Midland General.** Geoff Lumb

Below **City of Oxford converted some of its AEC Renowns for use as one-man buses, as illustrated by a 1965 vehicle in Aylesbury in 1970. Having the driver turn round to collect fares in the confined space of a half-width cab was not a great success, and one-man-operation of traditional half-cab 'deckers was rare.** Iain MacGregor

switched to Daimler Fleetlines in 1970. Pontypridd moved to single-deckers. Guy built a further batch of Arabs for Hong Kong in 1970, and later in the decade would produce front-engined Victory double-deckers for South Africa and Hong Kong.

There was still some limited interest in running half-cab double-deckers without conductors. Fleets such as Brighton and Eastern National did so using existing forward-entrance models. City of Oxford converted AEC Renowns for omo, after trying a Brighton Titan. Aberdeen tried half-cab omo buses too, and to do so rebuilt conventional open rear

platform Alexander-bodied CVG6s to forward-entrance layout. It planned to convert 10, but gave up after eight, with the conversions being carried out between 1968 and 1972.

The Aberdeen conversion was a major task. The lower saloon floor had to be extended to the rear of the bus and an emergency door fitted on the offside. A new rearward ascending staircase – built to the same dimensions as those in the Corporation's Fleetlines – was installed behind the driver's cab and a two-step entrance with double jack-knife electric doors fitted. The bonnet lid had to be reshaped so that it would not foul the re-

aligned front bulkhead window, and a periscope had to be fitted to give the driver a view of the upper saloon. On top of that the batteries were re-located and micro-switches fitted to the emergency doors to sound an alarm if they were opened.

The exercise reduced seating capacity from 66 to 64 and upped the unladen weight from 7 tons 9cwt to 7 tons 13cwt 3qrs. One practical problem of having the driver collect fares in a half-cab bus was that if any passengers, intentionally or otherwise, went straight upstairs without paying and then failed to hear (or heed) the driver's shouts, the hapless driver had to get out of his cab, walk round the front, and then go to the upper deck to get the offender to pay. It did happen, and it further delayed a service which was already slower than one which was crew-operated.

The conversion of rear-entrance double-deckers to forward entrance was rare indeed. The only other Scottish operator to try it was A1 of Ardrossan, which in 1964 had rebuilt an ex-London Transport RTL with a forward entrance.

Stockport Corporation's last PD3s were of forward-entrance layout and were intended for use as one-man buses, but this never happened. There was a slight cost penalty in buying forward-entrance vehicles and Stockport was one of very few fleets to buy a batch of buses featuring both layouts to provide a direct comparison. Its rear-entrance Titans delivered in 1969 cost £6,620 while the forward-entrance buses which accompanied them cost £6,923 – an extra five per cent. The added cost was all in the East Lancs bodies – the chassis for the forward-entrance buses were in fact slightly cheaper because they did not have a frame extension to support the rear platform and staircase.

There was a school of thought which – perhaps not surprisingly – had seen demand for double-deck buses in terminal decline. Many thought it unreasonable to expect the driver to collect 70-plus fares and were concerned about the time that would take. Others watched the strong trade union resistance to bigger buses and to one-man operation, and thought that to combine the two would simply not be possible.

This, plus the keen interest in single-deck operation by London and a number of other places such as Leeds, Liverpool and Sunderland, was a major factor in the formation in 1969 of the Leyland National Co. This was a joint venture between British Leyland and the newly-created National Bus Company, and its aim was to build a modern world-class integral single-decker. The genesis of the Leyland National was, incidentally, a 1966 mock-up of a four-axle single-decker which had used small wheels to achieve a low floor.

Yet by this time it should have been clear to Leyland's management that the double-deck might be making a come-back, although in fairness if they were to look at forward orders these still specified substantial numbers of rear-engined single-deckers – which would lead to a peak of around 1,300 deliveries in 1971, of which 360 were for London Transport and some 400 for NBC.

But among the Atlanteans and Fleetlines at the 1968 Commercial Motor Show, were trend-setting two-door buses for Manchester (the Mancunian) and Leeds (with panoramic-windowed Roe bodies) which were the first heralds of a double-deck revival. Park Royal showed its new standard on Atlanteans for Sheffield and Plymouth. In the demonstration park was an Alexander-bodied Atlantean for Newcastle with a nearside staircase. These, and others, were all designed for one-man-

operation and incorporated features such as periscopes to allow the driver to view the upper saloon (a legal requirement on omo double-deckers), and passenger counters on the stairs which could display the number of vacant seats on the top deck. Periscopes had to stay, but passenger counters were soon forgotten.

Although body styles were becoming increasingly standardised, there were still small numbers of bespoke bodies being built. The last East Lancs-bodied Atlanteans delivered to Bolton were of a unique style with sealed windows which had forward-sloping frames. Ventilation was provided by coach-style overhead jet-vents.

While the Leyland National project gathered momentum, another attempt to take advantage of the perceived growing market for single-deckers floundered. The Flxible Co (UK) was formed in 1968 with the intention of building US-style city buses. The project was backed by big names with former directors or

Rebuilding rear-entrance buses to forward-entrance was unusual – particularly so in the case of A1 of Ardrossan where the bus was a 15-year-old ex-London Transport RTL and there was no intention of running it without a conductor. The conversion was neat – and unique, in Britain at least. It increased the seating capacity from 56 to 57. Chris Aston

managers of Leyland, MCW and Plaxton linked to it. A left-hand-drive Flxible was brought to Britain, but the project quietly faded away.

Metro-Cammell, which felt threatened by the integral Leyland National and by Leyland's ownership of Park Royal and Roe and its links with ECW, forged an alliance with Swedish manufacturer Scania, to produce a UK version of the Scania CR110 city bus in Birmingham. This appeared as the Metro-Scania.

Into the 1970s

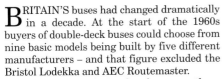

BAD MOON RISING

BRITAIN'S buses had changed dramatically in a decade. At the start of the 1960s buyers of double-deck buses could choose from nine basic models being built by five different manufacturers – and that figure excluded the Bristol Lodekka and AEC Routemaster.

In 1970 the choice lay between three models – Atlantean, Fleetline and VRT – from two manufacturers, British Leyland and Bristol, in which BL had a 50 per cent share.

A new Fleetline variant, the CRL6, under-scored the changes taking place, being powered by a Leyland O.680 engine and spelling the end of the PDR1/3 Atlantean with its drop-centre rear axle. The CRL6 was introduced in 1970; the last PDR1/3s entered service in 1971 and were 15 Alexander-bodied buses ordered for former BET subsidiaries East Midland and Western Welsh, although some of the Western Welsh buses were

diverted to East Yorkshire. A total of 81 PDR1/3s had been built over four years.

The rationalisation of chassis makers had not quite been matched amongst the bodybuilders. Most of the mainstream manu-facturers of double-deck bodies in 1960 were still active in 1970. The Weymann factory in Addlestone had closed in the spring of 1966, and Massey had been acquired by Northern Counties in 1967. But Alexander, East Lancs, Metro-Cammell (now known as Metro-Cammell Weymann), Northern Counties, Park Royal and Roe were all still active. Fringe manufacturers Longwell Green, Reading and Strachans had disappeared from double-deck production. Longwell Green had in fact ceased building bus bodies in 1966 with the delivery of two forward-entrance Regent Vs to Pontypridd. Reading's last double-decker, for Provincial, was built in 1967 and in the same

year Strachans' final double-deckers were delivered to Wolverhampton Corporation. The company would continue building single-deckers at its Hamble factory, but in decreasing numbers, until 1973.

The operating industry had changed too. Four Passenger Transport Executives had been created in England: Merseyside, SELNEC, Tyneside and West Midlands. They not only had the task of creating integrated public transport networks – they also had to modernise some of the fleets which they had inherited from the municipal bus undertak-ings they had absorbed. The National Bus Company was welding together the operations of the former Tilling and BET groups, and working out how best to handle its varied vehicle inheritance.

Front-engined double-deckers were being replaced as quickly as they reasonably could in fleets around the country, although in some places they enjoyed longer lives than they might otherwise have done as operators weeded out troublesome rear-engined single-deckers.

In London, AEC Merlins and Swifts were being replaced in the 1970s while RT-class AEC Regents, almost 20 years their senior, remained in all-day service. Almost without exception, operators running Daimler Roadliners withdrew them prematurely, which ensured the survival of older types. Rear-engined single-deckers from AEC and Leyland fared little better in some fleets, although most users of Swifts and Panthers persevered with them.

Urban single-deckers had, in most places, been adopted primarily as a means of intro-ducing one-man operation. The legalisation of double-deck omo effectively killed interest in rear-engined single-deckers in most fleets. London Transport had been the operator

The large Daimler badge fitted to Fleetlines and Roadliners was replaced by this smaller – and less expensive – style in 1968. Warrington Corporation took six Fleetlines in 1970 with East Lancs bodywork. The translucent roof panels were a popular feature around this time. *John Robinson*

This 1948 Guy Arab in the Provincial fleet, which had been bought from Southampton Corporation in 1965, was still in operation when the company was purchased by NBC in 1970. NBC was quick to replace elderly Guys with time-expired buses from other subsidiaries which were considerably younger than Provincial's oldest Guys. Iain MacGregor

which had embraced single-deck operation with the greatest enthusiasm. Indeed it had adopted the concept with unseemly haste, and its disenchantment also came quickly.

So in 1970 the first of a new generation of London double-deckers was unveiled: the DMS, briefly and unconvincingly named the Londoner. Manchester general manager Ralph Bennett had moved to London Transport in 1968, and with the Londoner no doubt hoped to repeat the success of the Mancunian in his previous post. But it was a name which didn't catch on, and the buses to which it was applied would soon be criticised almost as much as the single-deckers they were replacing.

The DMS was a Daimler Fleetline with dual-door bodywork, initially by Park Royal, but from 1972 also by Metro-Cammell. The styling was in the angular idiom of the time, but in all-over red it looked plain when compared with vehicles like the Mancunian, or even standard Park Royal bodies for fleets such as East Kent or Sheffield, with their brighter liveries. LT's initial order called for 17 Fleetlines for delivery in 1969, a number which was quickly increased, and although the first didn't enter service until early 1971, by 1973 there would be over 1,000 in operation.

Among some of the former BET companies

there was still strong interest in high-capacity single-deckers. Maidstone & District had built up a fleet of 95 Leyland Panthers between 1965 and 1968 and in 1970 added 30 Daimler Fleetline SRG6LX/36. They had dual-door Marshall bodies. But most were soon moved on to other former BET companies in exchange for double-deckers, and further Willowbrook-bodied buses due in 1972 were diverted to Northern General before delivery. Northern General already had SRG6LX/36s in operation having taken 24 with Alexander W-type bodies in 1971. They were to have been accompanied by 52 Bristol RELL6Gs with two-door ECW bodies, although in the end only 23 were delivered, with the remainder being diverted to United Auto and also to Provincial, where they helped to speed replacement of that company's unusual Deutz-engined Guy rebuilds and other assorted ageing Arabs, reminders of the days when the company had been one of the more individualistic independents. It had been purchased by NBC at the start of 1970. PMT ran 21 long Fleetline single-deckers with Alexander bodies.

The use of the Atlantean chassis as the basis of a single-decker, first tried by Great Yarmouth in 1967, was revived in 1970–71.

Portsmouth Corporation took 12 long-wheelbase PDR2/1s with 40-seat two-door Seddon bodies. These followed earlier deliveries of Panther Cubs and AEC Swifts, and provided some standardisation with the fleet's double-deckers. Portsmouth had been buying Atlanteans since 1963.

The only other user of single-deck Atlanteans (excluding later rebuilds of double-deckers) was the Merseyside PTE. It took delivery of two 40-seat dual-door Northern Counties-bodied PDR2/1s in 1970. These had been ordered by Birkenhead Corporation which had been buying Atlantean double-deckers since 1968.

Not all operators were convinced that rear-engined double-deckers and one-man operation made a good combination. There was a belief that one-man buses were driven harder, and that drivers were therefore less likely to be paying much attention to potentially expensive problems developing in an engine which they couldn't hear (or, in extreme circumstances, smell). The belief was often justified as many operators failed to recognise the amount of time taken at stops collecting fares and thus ran omo buses to schedules which were little different from those used for crew-operation.

Above **The Tynesider was an attempt by Northern General to create a double-decker suitable for one-man-operation but without the problems – cost and reduced reliability – associated with rear-engined designs. It was a major rebuild of a rear-entrance Metro-Cammell-bodied Leyland Titan PD3 – see photograph on page 24 – and in its new form seated 68 with a wide entrance immediately behind the front wheel. It was little used.** David Little

Below **After rebuilding a Titan, Northern General turned its hand to a forward-entrance Routemaster which had suffered front-end accident damage. While still a major job, the rebuild was not as extensive as that on the Titan and mainly involved relocating the driving position to put the driver nearer the door.** Alan Mortimer

Northern General's chief engineer, David Cox, was one of those with reservations and in 1972 Northern General rebuilt a 1958 Metro-Cammell-bodied PD3 to normal-control layout. This was the Tynesider, and by having the entrance directly opposite the driver was intended to be an ideal one-man-operated double-decker. However it saw little use. This was a prelude to the similar rebuild of an accident-damaged Routemaster which was christened the Wearsider, but it too was little used.

There was also continuing general dissatisfaction with rear-engined double-deckers in some quarters, aside from any problems associated with running them as one-man buses. They were more complex than front-engined models, which meant increased time in the workshops and the need for a greater number of spare buses, costs which operators hadn't really expected but which they now couldn't really avoid.

In its 1970 annual report, NBC complained: "The disquiet of bus operators about the reliability of the modern double-deck bus constructed to the standards laid down by the Department of the Environment was expressed on a number of occasions in 1970. Though British-built buses are, by comparison with what is available from overseas manufacturers, still relatively good value, they do not compare well in reliability with earlier British designs. In one company alone, the high incidence of breakdown has necessitated substantial modifications to a fleet of 300 new vehicles. In a number of cases the refurbishing of old but reliable vehicles for a further seven years' service has been preferred and proved satisfactory."

The Scottish Bus Group at around the same time noted that double-deck buses "with engine, gearbox and transmission all located at the rear, are still subject to an unduly high rate of mechanical failure, but at present there is no alternative available on the British market. Until the Group can obtain dependable double-deckers, intake is being confined to a minimum and replacement taken alternatively in underfloor, large-seating capacity single deck buses."

Ultimately the most extreme dissatisfaction was voiced by SBG which, it might be noted, had avoided all of the low-floor rear-engined single-deck models (apart from buying a dozen Bristol RELLs for Alexander Fife). In 1968–69 SBG had bought 109 Bristol VRTs for four of its fleets: Alexander Midland, Central SMT, Scottish Omnibuses and Western SMT. Such was the level of their unreliability that all but three (which were sold elsewhere) went south to NBC in 1973–74 in exchange for Bristol Lodekkas. Early VRTs suffered from cooling problems and transmission failures. In time, of course, SBG would be responsible for the re-invention of the front-

Right **The flat windscreens on ECW bodies on rear-engined chassis created reflections at night which impeded the driver's vision, and ECW adapted its bodywork to take the BET-style windscreen, as seen on a 1972 Fleetline for Yorkshire Woollen District. There were 12 in all, and they were the last buses to be delivered in the company's dark red; subsequent new buses would be in NBC poppy red.** Martin Llewellyn

Below right **While the front-engined half-cab bus effectively died in 1969 as far as British operators were concerned, one came to play an unlikely role in helping Dennis to develop a new rear-engined model in the mid-1970s. This one-time Leeds City Transport Daimler CVG6LX/30, new in 1959, was bought by Dennis in 1975 to test the compatibility of the Gardner 6LXB engine with a Voith automatic gearbox – the combination it planned to use in its new model. Among the operators who put it to the test in 1976–77 was London Transport, where it ran alongside Routemasters on a lengthy cross-London route in the summer of 1977. It had Roe bodywork.** Stewart J Brown

engined double-decker in the shape of the Ailsa.

The Lodekka exchange was the last major half-cab event in the UK. SBG's impatience with its troublesome VRTs might have been echoed with other models in other fleets, but none went to the extreme of replacing them with older half-cabs.

Rising labour costs were making crew operation expensive. Most operators got rid of conductors as quickly as they reasonably could. One-man – or, gradually, one-person – operation was the future and in most fleets it could not happen quickly enough. A measure of the rapid progress being made can be seen at NBC where the percentage of local bus miles operated by one-man-buses doubled from 25 to 50 between 1969 and 1971 partly through the delivery of new buses and partly by converting suitable older buses. The Government's new bus grant helped fund rapid fleet replacement and even in the second-hand market elderly half-cabs were no longer a popular buy. Many of the small independent fleets which had traditionally bought second-hand double-deckers were instead buying new Fords and Bedfords, with the cost being under-written by the new bus grant. By the close of the 1970s, half-cab double-deckers would be rare outside London.

One withdrawn half-cab which received an unexpected new lease of life was a former Leeds City Transport Daimler. In the mid-1970s Dennis was contemplating re-entering the bus market with a rear-engined double-deck chassis which would use a Gardner engine and a Voith gearbox. These were proven products on their own, but not in combination. The answer was to install a Voith gearbox in an ex-Leeds Daimler CVG6LX/30 which then acted as a mobile test-bed in

service with a few operators, including London Transport, for whom it was repainted red.

While the writing was on the wall for the half-cab from the day the first Atlantean entered service, it took a decade to convince all operators that rear-engined buses were the way forward. Britain's biggest operator, London Transport, having backed the sophisticated Routemaster, was among those

slow to change. But there's a pleasant irony in the fact that the Routemaster is the only half-cab design still in regular all-day service in the new millennium. London Transport as a bus operator has gone, and the influence of its successors on vehicle designers and manufacturers is nowhere near that of LT in its heyday – but LT's spirit lived on in the 596 Routemasters licensed for service in the capital which made it to the new millennium.

Half Cab . . .

APPENDIX

That there are lies, damned lies and statistics there can be no doubt – but the statistics in the accompanying tables are a fair representation of the deliveries of new double-deck buses by make and model to UK fleets in the postwar period up to 1969. They have been collated drawing on a wide range of sources, sometimes conflicting, but they do illustrate how each manufacturer performed over a period of time, and how manufacturers' sales compared at any given point in time.

The primary sources of data were PSV Circle fleet histories and chassis lists, and acknowledgement is made of the debt enthusiasts owe to the hard work put in by the PSV Circle and its members, over many years, in recording the vehicles operated by bus companies in Britain and abroad.

Not included in these figures are exports (including those to the Irish Republic) and rebodied vehicles.

Deliveries of new double-deckers to United Kingdom operators: 1946–1969 Figures in red indicate the best selling models for each year.

		1946	1947	1948	1949	1950	1951	1952	1953	1954	1955	1956	1957	1958	1959	1960	1961	1962	1963	1964	1965	1966	1967	1968	1969
AEC	Regent	305	546	1430	1441	1653	994	678	684	557	198	517	361	157	93	182	153	156	235	131	65	70	52	3	2
	Routemaster	—	—	—	—	—	—	—	—	—	1	—	2	1	183	440	441	384	347	336	302	236	193	10	—
	Bridgemaster	—	—	—	—	—	—	—	—	—	—	2	2	14	37	24	50	28	28	—	—	—	—	—	—
	Renown	—	—	—	—	—	—	—	—	—	—	—	—	—	—	—	—	—	57	48	95	46	5	—	—
Albion	Venturer	—	20	52	69	50	3	—	25	—	—	—	—	—	—	—	—	—	—	—	—	—	—	—	—
	Lowlander	—	—	—	—	—	—	—	—	—	—	—	—	—	—	—	—	21	212	22	13	5	1	—	—
Atkinson		—	—	—	—	—	—	—	—	1	—	—	—	—	—	—	—	—	—	—	—	—	—	—	—
BMMO		—	—	—	70	51	71	8	50	100	50	50	100	1	—	50	46	50	50	99	10	41	—	—	—
Bristol	K	264	224	449	499	450	229	367	298	122	50	10	35	—	—	—	—	—	—	—	—	—	—	—	—
	Lodekka	—	—	—	1	1	—	—	—	6	184	373	435	305	365	356	352	359	476	398	382	465	401	287	71	—
	VR	—	—	—	—	—	—	—	—	—	—	—	—	—	—	—	—	—	—	—	2	—	28	213
Crossley	DD42	186	137	271	205	265	35	14	—	—	—	—	—	—	—	—	—	—	—	—	—	—	—	—	—
Daimler	CW/CV	330	350	441	551	373	438	263	230	255	160	219	316	127	147	50	86	102	168	114	71	72	8	8	—
	Fleetline	—	—	—	—	—	—	—	—	—	—	—	—	—	1	11	113	386	412	395	386	476	540	534
Dennis	Lance	—	9	—	29	22	3	5	—	32	—	—	—	—	—	—	—	—	—	—	—	—	—	—	—
	Loline	—	—	—	—	—	—	—	—	—	—	1	38	5	45	44	66	—	33	34	8	5	—	—	—
Foden	PVD	—	11	13	5	5	12	2	—	3	1	5	—	—	—	—	—	—	—	—	—	—	—	—	—
Guy	Arab	228	69	134	229	351	230	222	225	105	153	204	158	87	33	35	81	27	75	44	63	65	59	—	6
	Wulfrunian	—	—	—	—	—	—	—	—	—	—	—	—	—	1	11	47	13	34	—	30	—	—	—	—
Leyland	Titan	447	902	1137	1685	1674	896	415	546	573	431	572	594	926	483	374	497	404	321	263	227	169	201	74	19
	Atlantean	—	—	—	—	—	—	—	1	1	—	1	—	4	260	373	188	347	412	293	461	505	373	387	540
Total motorbuses		1760	2268	3927	4784	4895	2911	1974	2065	1932	1418	2015	1874	1720	1598	1937	2003	2187	2723	2177	2231	2006	1660	1121	1314
BUT		—	6	143	112	182	35	75	3	35	61	35	17	70	3	—	—	—	—	—	—	—	—	—	—
Crossley		—	—	—	20	23	18	—	—	—	—	—	—	—	—	—	—	—	—	—	—	—	—	—	—
Daimler		—	—	—	—	25	5	—	—	—	—	—	—	—	—	—	—	—	—	—	—	—	—	—	—
Guy		—	1	23	94	2	—	—	—	—	—	—	—	—	—	—	—	—	—	—	—	—	—	—	—
Karrier		45	21	35	30	—	—	—	—	—	—	—	—	—	—	—	—	—	—	—	—	—	—	—	—
Sunbeam		55	38	92	80	63	30	12	33	15	15	7	—	20	21	8	12	9	—	—	—	—	—	—	—
Total trolleybuses		100	66	293	336	295	88	87	36	50	76	42	17	90	24	8	12	9	—	—	—	—	—	—	—
Total double-deck		1860	2334	4220	5120	5190	2999	2061	2101	1982	1494	2057	1891	1810	1622	1945	2015	2196	2723	2177	2231	2006	1660	1121	1314

United Kingdom double-deck bus deliveries: 1946–1969 — Manufacturers' market shares

Note: Percentages have been rounded to the nearest whole number, so figures do not always total 100.

	1946	1947	1948	1949	1950	1951	1952	1953	1954	1955	1956	1957	1958	1959	1960	1961	1962	1963	1964	1965	1966	1967	1968	1969
AEC	16	23	34	28	32	33	33	33	28	13	25	19	10	19	33	32	26	25	22	21	18	15	1	0
Bristol	14	10	11	10	9	8	18	15	15	28	22	18	20	22	18	18	22	15	18	21	20	17	9	16
Daimler	18	15	11	11	7	15	13	11	13	11	11	17	7	9	3	5	10	20	24	21	23	29	49	41
Guy	12	3	3	4	7	8	11	11	5	10	10	8	5	2	2	6	2	4	2	4	3	4	0	0
Leyland	24	39	27	33	32	30	20	26	29	29	28	31	51	46	38	34	35	35	27	31	34	35	41	43
Other motorbuses	10	8	8	7	8	4	1	4	7	4	3	5	2	0	5	5	6	2	6	2	2	0	0	0
Trolleybuses	5	3	7	7	6	3	4	2	3	5	2	1	5	1	0	1	0	0	0	0	0	0	0	0

The switch to rear-engines: Percentages of new front- and rear-engined double-deckers delivered to United Kingdom operators: 1958–1970

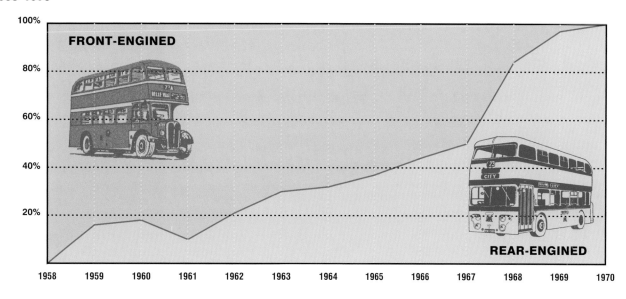

Deliveries of new double-deckers: 1946–1969

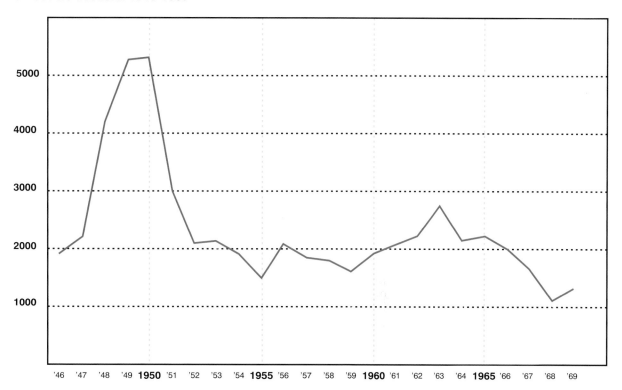

Scots find them thrifty

Edinburgh's 60-seater Titans average 10·53 M.P.G

A new and remarkable story of low-cost transport operation has been started in Edinburgh where 100 Leyland 'Titan' double-deckers are replacing the existing tramway system. These new buses, with M.C.W. bodies, weigh only 6 tons 12 cwts. unladen, and are powered by Leyland 125 h.p. diesels. Fuel consumption, checked after 76,604 miles, revealed the startlingly low figure of 10.53 miles a gallon, on multiple-stop city service. Even with this exceptionally low fuel consumption, the reserve of power of the large engine will enable faster schedules to be operated and so make these 'Titans' the most desirable units ever produced for city operation.

Leyland 60 seater 'TITAN'

LEYLAND MOTORS LTD. Head Office & Works : LEYLAND LANCS ENGLAND
London Office & Export Division : HANOVER HOUSE, HANOVER SQUARE, LONDON, W.1.